BRAIN GAMES ®

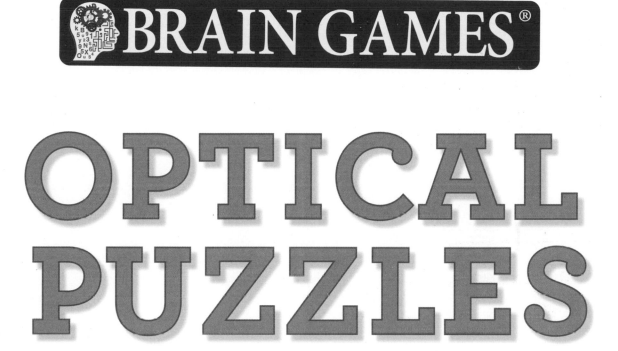

OPTICAL PUZZLES

pil

Publications International, Ltd.

Cover creator: Cihan Altay, Philip Carter, Barry Clarke, Connie Formby, Grabarchuk Family, Robin Humer, Gianni Sarcone, Shavan R. Spears, Terry Stickels, Jen Torche

Puzzle Illustrator: Helem An, Connie Formby, Robin Humer, Jessi LeDonne, Nicole H. Lee, Jay Sato, Shavan R. Spears, Jen Torche

Louis Weber, CEO
Publications International, Ltd.
8140 Lehigh Avenue
Morton Grove, Illinois 60053

ISBN: 978-1-68022-529-7

Manufactured in China.

8 7 6 5 4 3 2 1

AN EYEFUL OF (AQUEOUS) HUMOR

Our human eyes and brains want to make sense of the world around us. We complete our own mental pictures of characters in books or fill in details that aren't explained during even bad movies. Somehow, bright cumulus clouds become images of animals or objects or scenes from our lives. In fact, our eyes constantly gloss over their own small built-in blind spot — called a scotoma, and everyone has them — where the eyeball connects. Humans always want to have more complete information!

Optical illusions play on this urge in the human brain and also trick our visual perceptions. Instead of seeing the harsh shadow left behind by bright headlights or a too-sunny day, why not use the idea of an afterimage to create a fun puzzle? Suddenly a dark, dreary version of the American flag turns into the proper colors when we look away. Our eyes swim with perceived motion after we stare at a swirling spiral.

In *Brain Games®: Optical Puzzles*, you'll find a diverse mix of more than 135 visual illusions and activities. Use your own colors to make classic "impossible objects" come to life. Turn pages sideways and upside-down to find hidden meanings and perspectives. Solve spatial puzzles by using logic and your imagination. The variety will keep you guessing, at least until you check your answers at the back of the book!

Some classic types of illusions have been explained or at least strongly theorized about by scientists, but others are still a mystery — why do our eyes behave this way? The lack of explanations has never stopped those who find these illusions fun to make and view. We love to suspend our disbelief, the same way we do when we watch a magician or even a scary movie. And it's fun and thought-provoking to prod the edges of the ways our eyes can fool us.

If this horse seems to have a few human characteristics, it's no coincidence. Flip this page over and find out why!

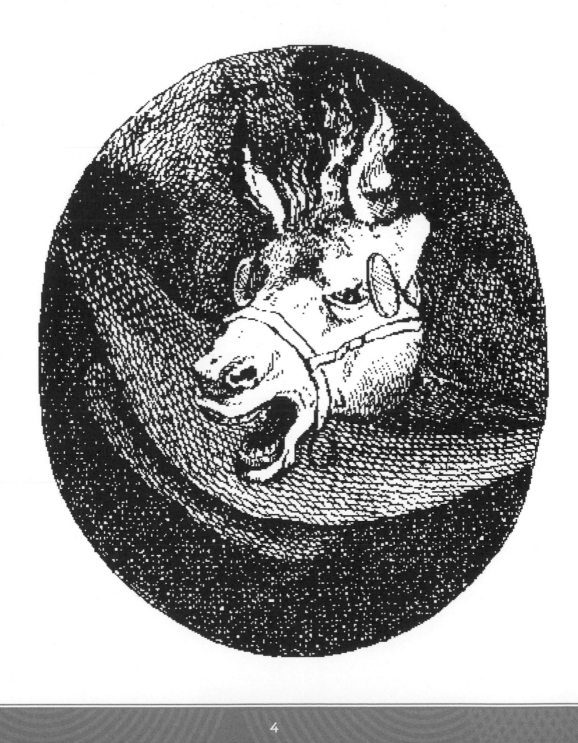

ALTERNATE CORNERS

Draw a single closed loop passing through each cell of the grid exactly once and moving only horizontally and vertically. Every second corner of the loop is on a circle, and each circle is a corner. Every other corner is on an empty cell.

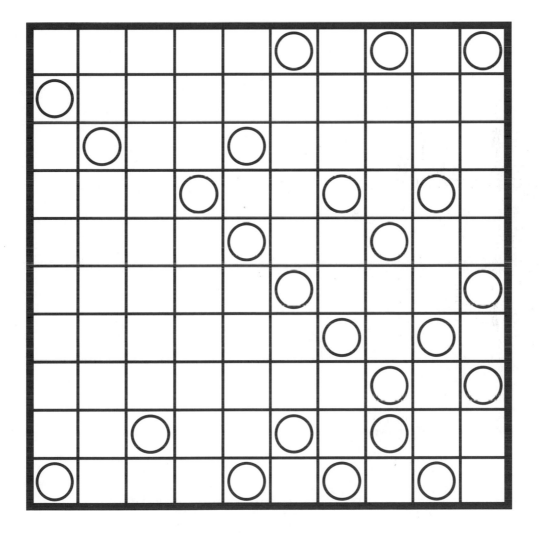

Answer on page 144.

Complete the optical illusion and make it pop by coloring the areas that correspond to the numbers in the color key. Use our color suggestions, a light-medium-dark combination of your own, or any other three colors you like.

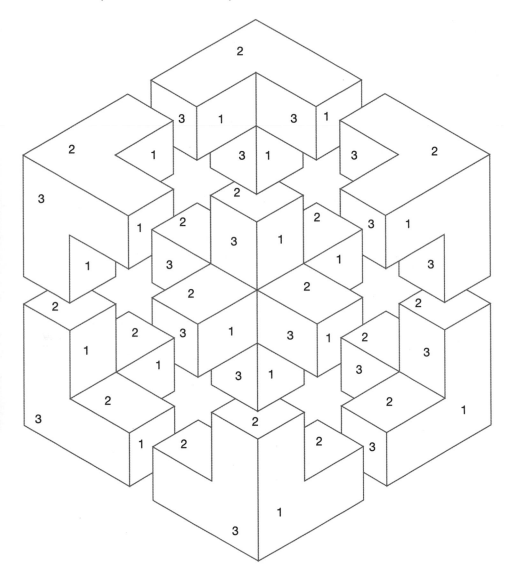

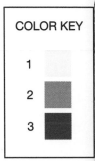

COLOR KEY

1

2

3

Answer on page 144.

SQUARE HOLDINGS

Which of the 2 interior squares are exactly the same?

Answer on page 144.

ALOHA!

There are 2 errors hidden in the image of the hula girl. Can you spot them both?

Answer on page 144.

MONDRIANIZE IT!

Inspired by the artwork of Belgian artist Piet Mondrian, these puzzles consist of stars and circles. Using the checkered pattern as a guide, draw in lines so that each star is in its own square, and each circle in its own rectangle.

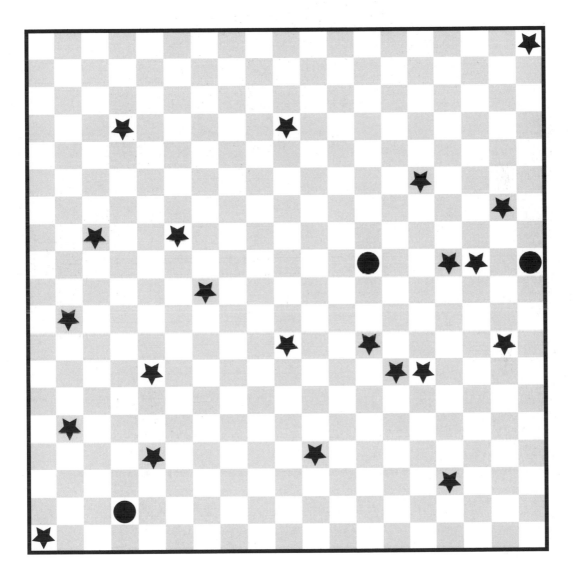

Answer on page 144.

Are the octagons within the Yin-Yang symbol the same color?

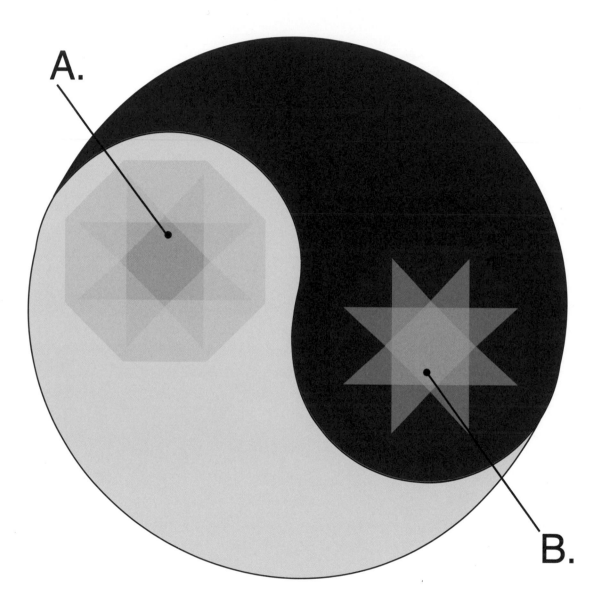

Answer on page 145.

Someone isn't finding this Sunday's sermon all that interesting. In fact, it's put him to sleep. Can you find the snoozing worshiper?

Answer on page 145.

Study the dice—which red dot is bigger?

Answer on page 145.

Which one of the cubes can be made from the unfolded sample?

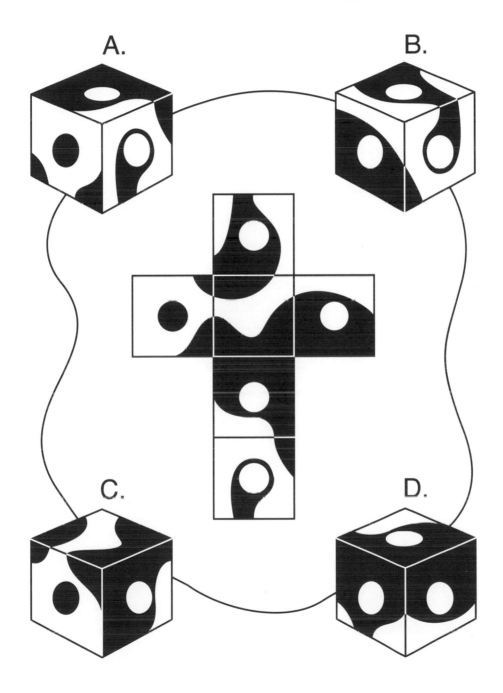

A.

B.

C.

D.

Answer on page 145.

WARPED GRID

With the help of some carefully placed white squares, it appears that a circle is rising from this grid. The reality is that a circular shape is only suggested: Your mind fills in the gaps.

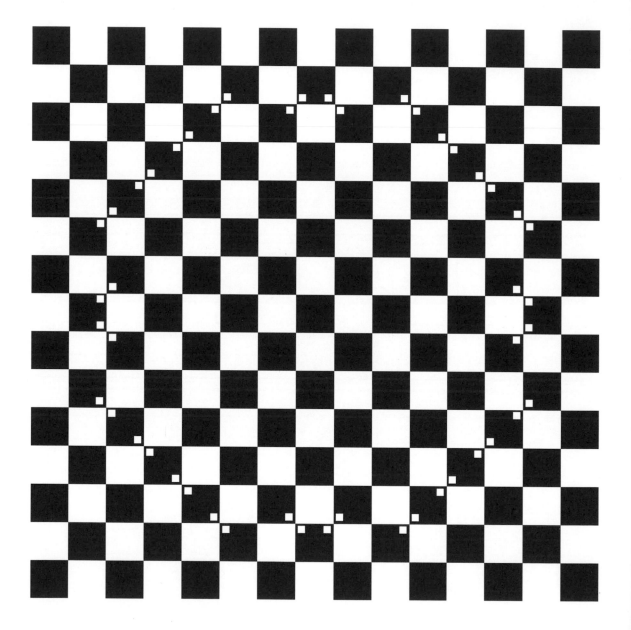

STEPPING STONES

Complete the optical illusion and make it pop by coloring the areas that correspond to the numbers in the color key. Use our color suggestions, a light-medium-dark combination of your own, or any other three colors you like.

COLOR KEY

1

2

3

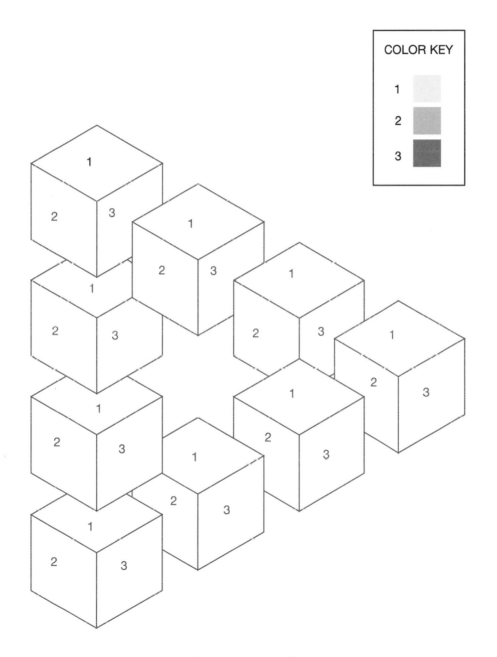

Answer on page 145.

COLORED IN?

Although the continents and surrounding water appeared to be shaded in (with colors orange and blue, respectively), they are in fact uniformly white! The color sensation is caused by the contrasting color outlines.

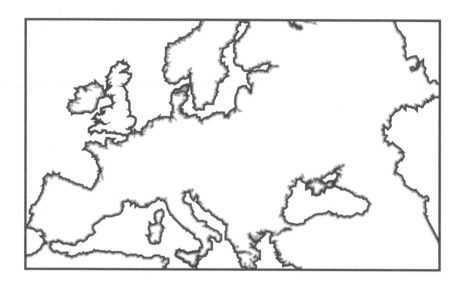

ARROW WEB

Shade in some of the arrows so that each arrow in the grid points to exactly one shaded arrow.

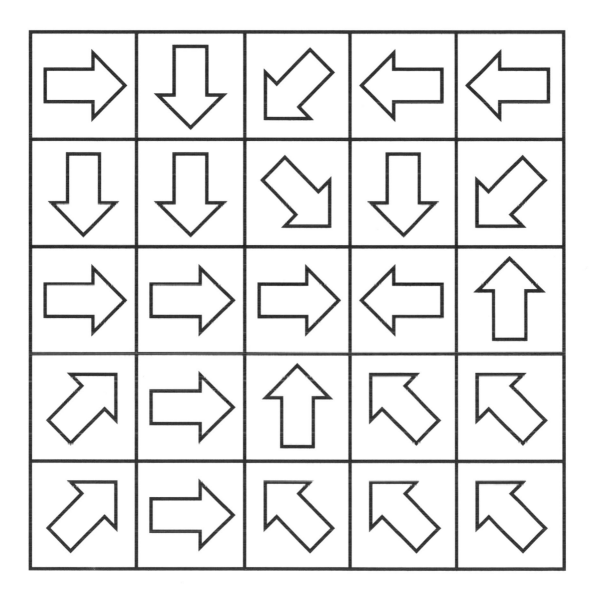

Answer on page 145.

A structure like this cannot exist in the 3D world.

Located in this barnyard scene is the shepherd. Can you find him?

Answer on page 146.

Which of the lettered figures continues the sequence?

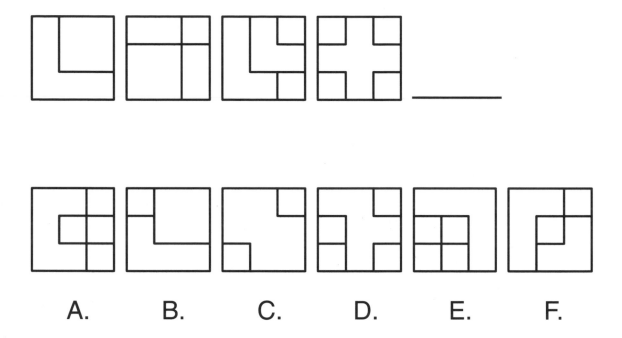

A.   B.   C.   D.   E.   F.

Answer on page 146.

Which line, A or B, is connected to C?

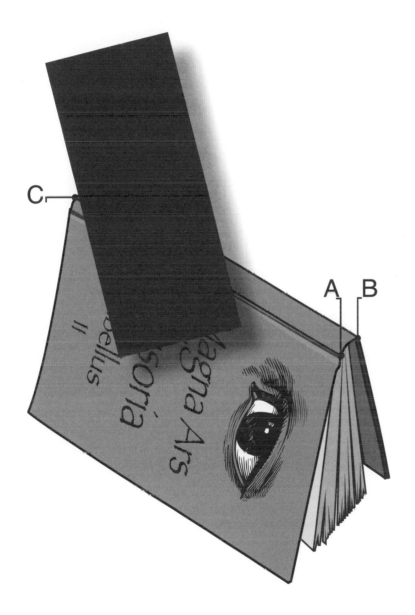

Answer on page 146.

By readjusting some lines in this pattern, it appears that a circle is rising from within.

Complete the optical illusion and make it pop by coloring the areas that correspond to the numbers in the color key. Use our color suggestions, a light-medium-dark combination of your own, or any other three colors you like.

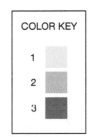

COLOR KEY

1

2

3

Answer on page 146.

Oops! Four mugshots accidentally got sent through the shredder, and Officer Cuse is trying to straighten them out. Currently, only one facial feature in each row is in its correct place. Officer Cuse knows that:

     1. C's eyes are one place to the right of his hair and 2 places to the right of D's nose.

     2. A's mouth is one place ot the right of B's eyes and one place to the left of D's hair.

     3. C's mouth is 2 places to the left of his nose.

     4. B's hair is one place to the right of C's eyes.

Can you find the correct hair, eyes, nose, and mouth for each person?

Answer on page 146.

FIND THE LOVERS

Ah, young love. So many times it has to stay hidden. In this case, the clandestine affair is literal. Find the kissing couple in the illustration below.

Answer on page 146.

PARADE'S ROUTE

The parade starts at the northwest corner, visits each street corner exactly once and ends at the southeast corner on the map of the town square. Find the parade's route.

Start

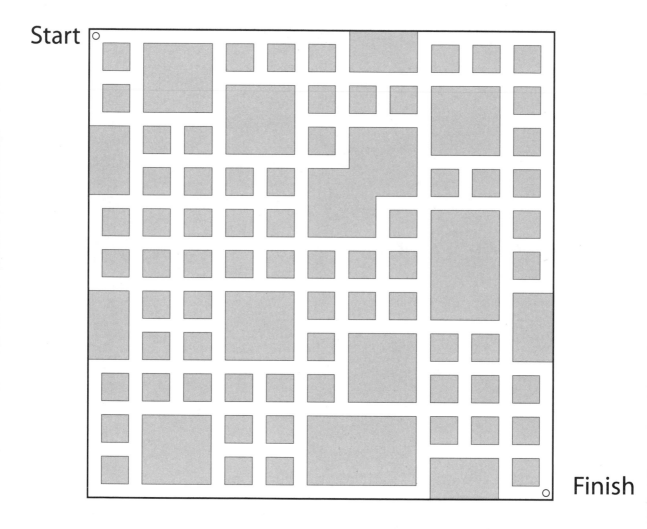

Finish

Answer on page 147.

STRAIGHT LINES

Stare at this image, and the lines passing through the circle will appear to bend. They are perfectly straight—this is an illusion caused by the rings the lines pass through.

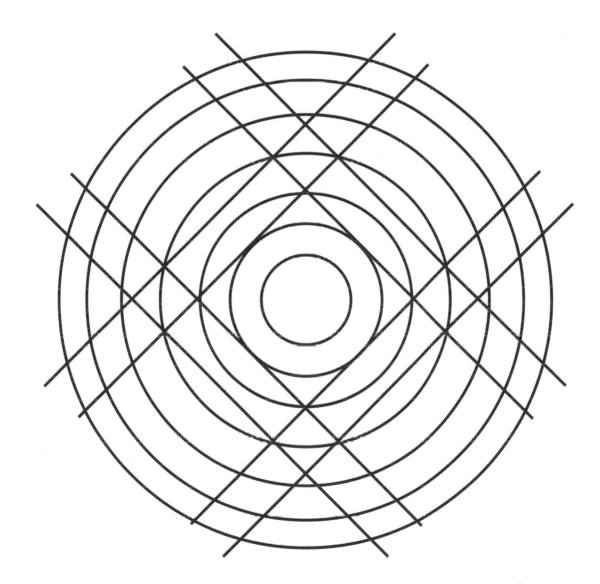

Which line is longer, the one surrounded by the arrows facing in, or the one where the arrows are facing out?

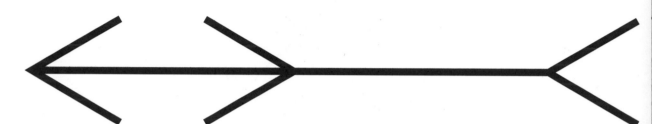

Answer on page 147.

If at least some segments of each side of a triangle pass through a square, what is the maximum number of distinct areas, not further subdivided, that could result?

A. 4
B. 7
C. 11
D. 17

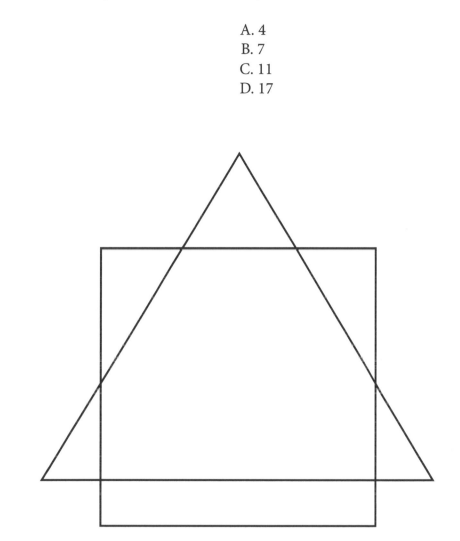

Answer on page 147.

TRIANGLES GALORE

Triangles are pointed in every direction. How many can you count?

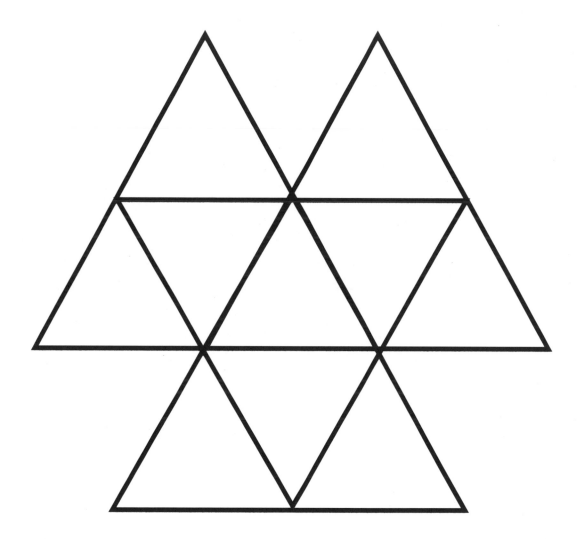

Answer on page 147.

GET SOME PERSPECTIVE

This what happens when perspective goes awry—this block illustration has no vanishing point, and thus no clear perspective.

OPTICAL PUZZLES

Complete the optical illusion and make it pop by coloring the areas that correspond to the numbers in the color key. Use our color suggestions or any other three colors you like.

Answer on page 147.

TURN THAT SMILE UPSIDE DOWN

Like many other illusions, this image gives you one thing while keeping another out of sight. At least sight in the sense of how we're accustomed to looking at things. Turn this page upside down, and you'll turn those grins around as well.

TOTALLY CUBULAR!

What do you see here? Cubes? Rectangles? The number 6? The number 9?

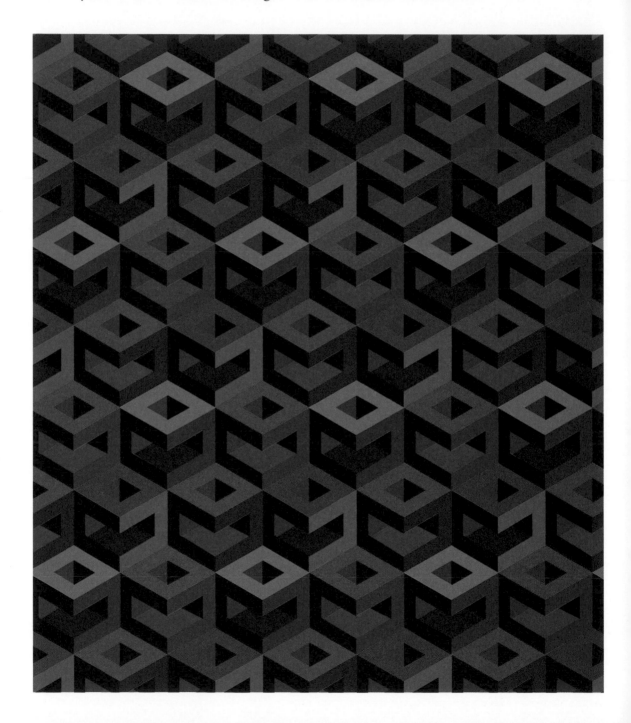

FLOWER GROWTH

Which of these flowers has the longest stem?

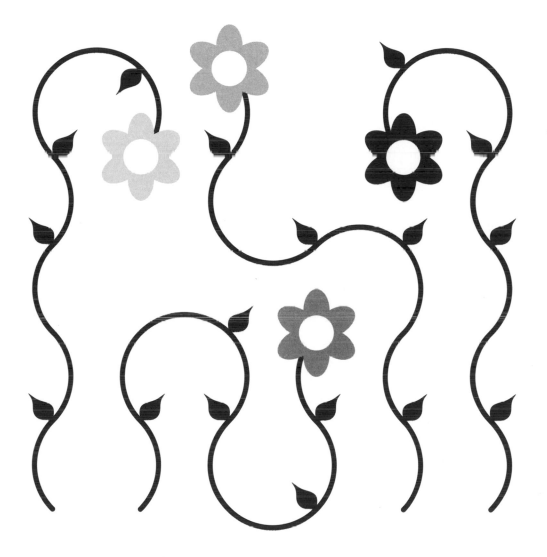

Answer on page 147.

Which is wider, the H or the W?

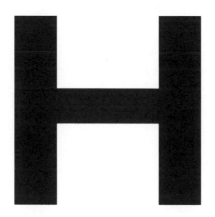

Answer on page 148.

The squares fold in on themselves until collapsing at the center.

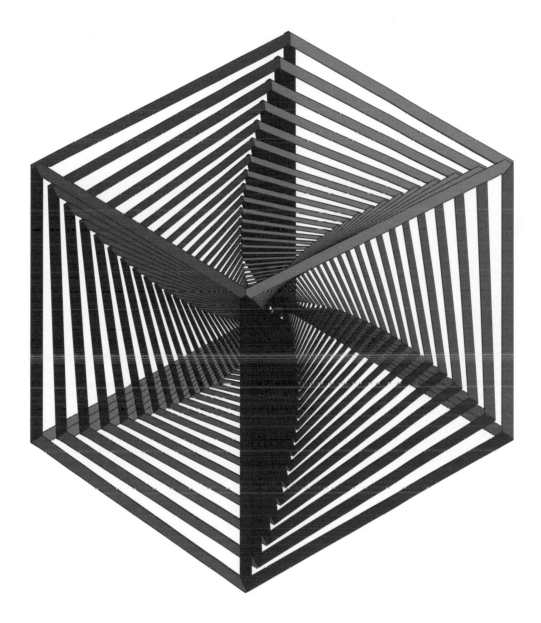

The 3-D figure consists of 8 cubes. If you could pick this up and turn it around, how many square outlines of all possible sizes would you be able to recognize on the entire figure?

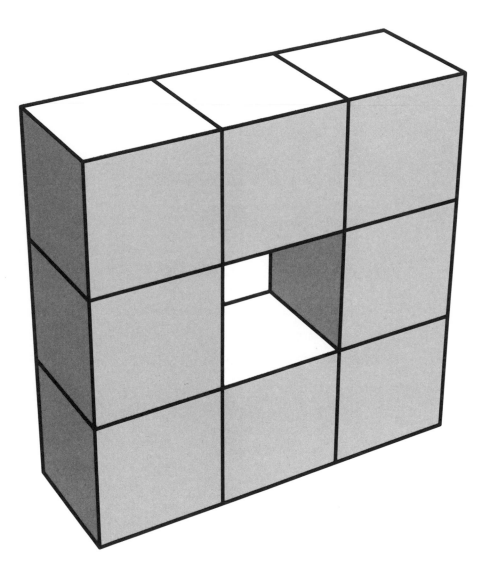

Answer on page 148.

Complete the optical illusion and make it pop by coloring the areas that correspond to the numbers in the color key. Use our color suggestions or any other three colors you like.

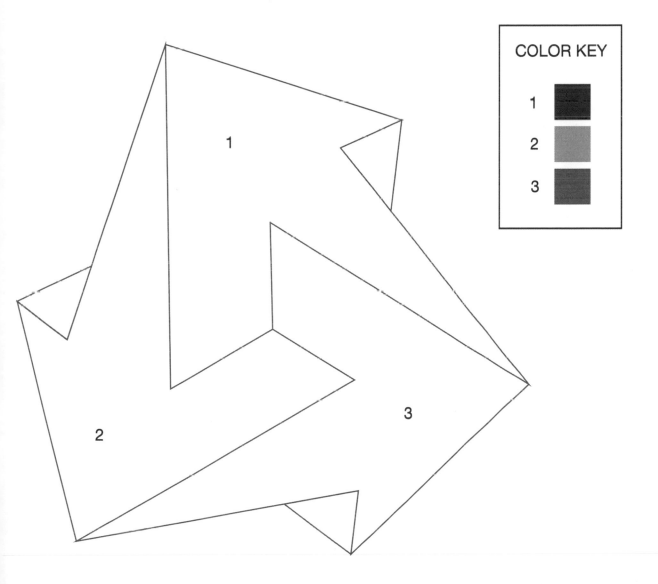

COLOR KEY

1

2

3

Answer on page 148.

Another shape that, while looking correct at first glance, is actually impossible to create.

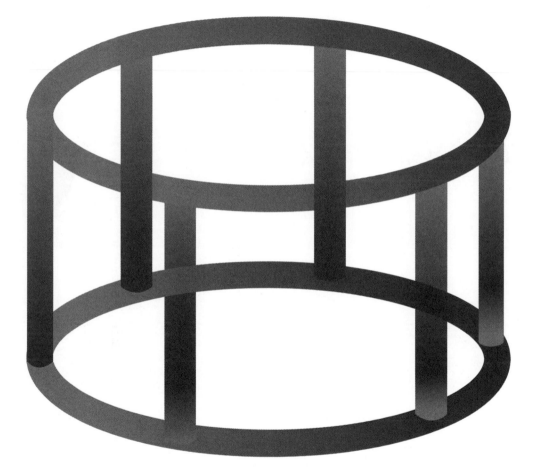

UP IN SMOKE

There's a thief in this man's midst—and he's stolen his best cigars! See if you can focus your visual acuity and spot the cigar thief.

Answer on page 148.

MONDRIANIZE IT!

Inspired by the artwork of Belgian artist Piet Mondrian, these puzzles consist of stars and circles. Using the checkered pattern as a guide, draw in lines so that each star is in its own square, and each circle in its own rectangle.

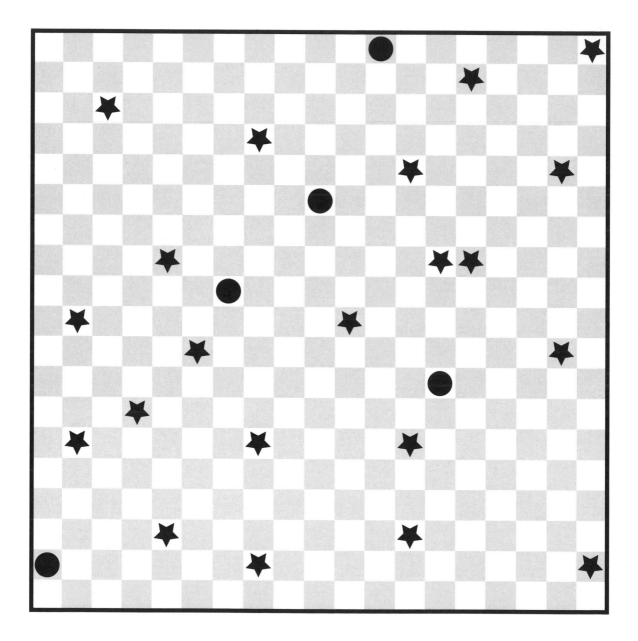

Answer on page 148.

Move your head back and forth while focusing on these circles. They appear to shift with your movements.

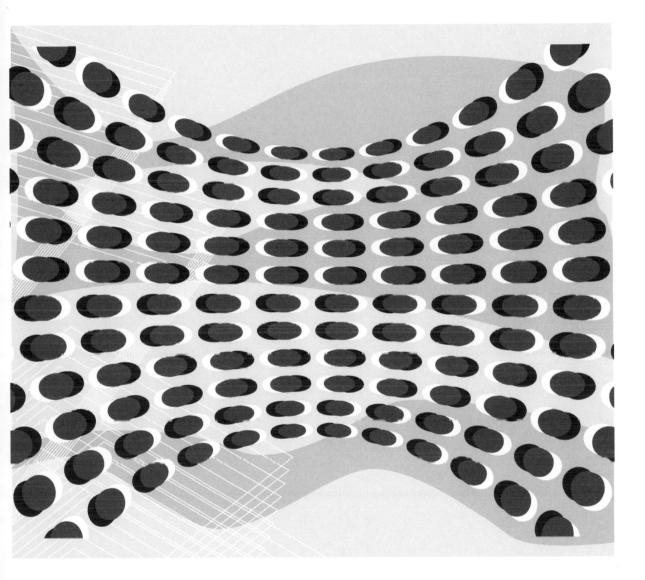

The box appears to have depth; the circle inside it appears to have shape. But, this is only a manipulation of space and dimension!

SUPERNOVA

Stare closely—but not too closely—at this color explosion, and watch the colors ripple back and forth.

OPTICAL PUZZLES

Complete the optical illusion and make it pop by coloring the areas that correspond to the numbers in the color key. Use our color suggestions, a light-medium-dark combination of your own, or any other three colors you like.

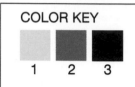

COLOR KEY
1　2　3

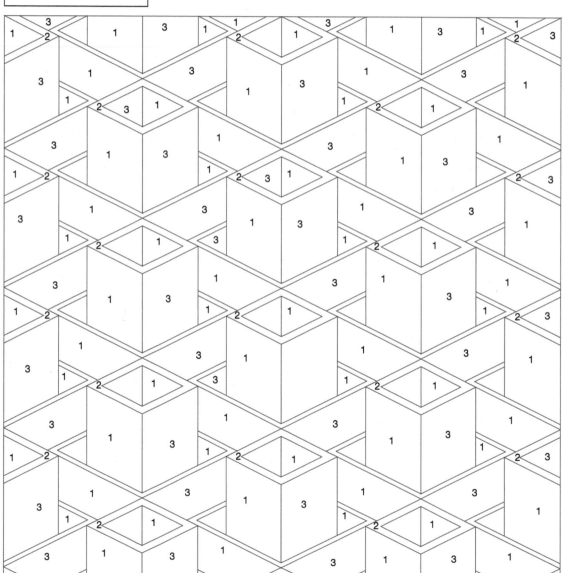

Answer on page 149.

DON'T GET OUTFOXED

Hidden in this tranquil scene is an outline of a fox. Can you find it?

Answer on page 149.

Which one of the cubes is a correct wrap of the center pattern?

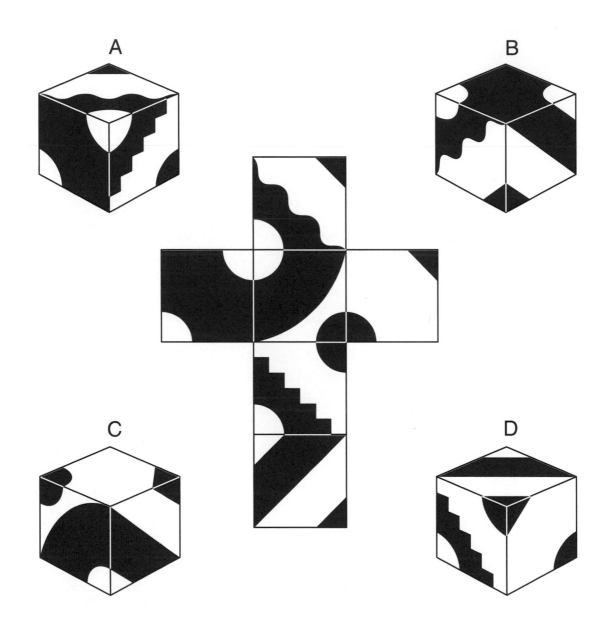

Answer on page 149.

WINDING ABYSS

Stare deeply into this image; the circles appear to spiral in toward the middle, even though they remain in straight rows.

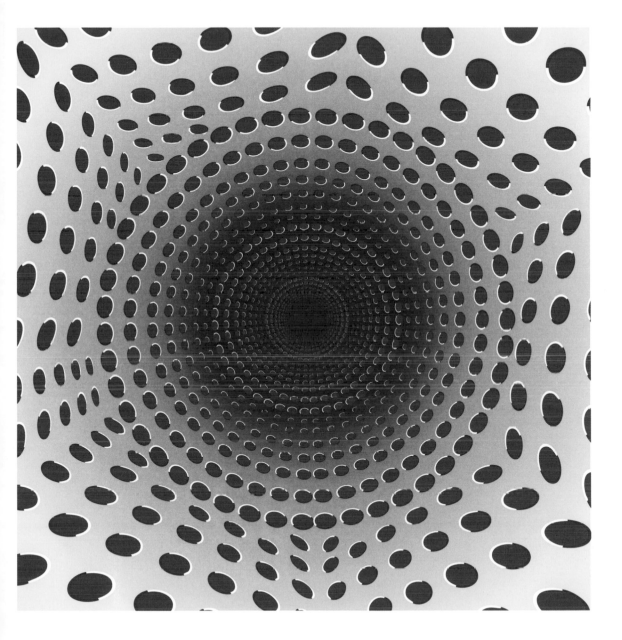

Complete the optical illusion and make it pop by coloring the areas that correspond to the number in the color key. Use our color suggestion or any other color you like.

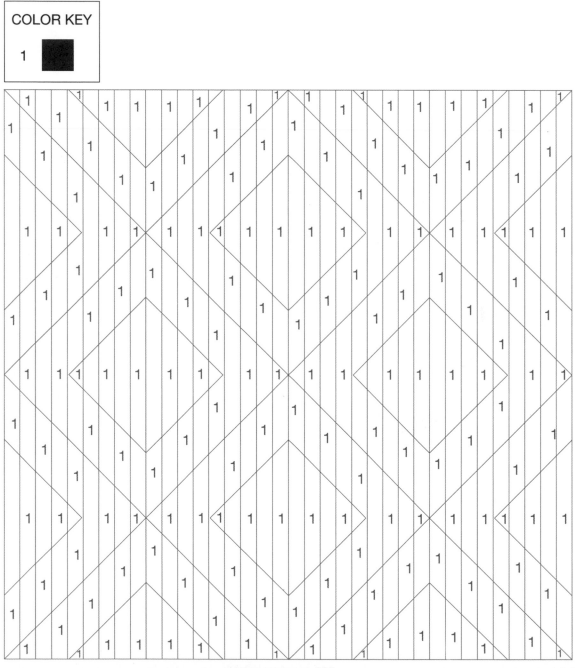

Answer on page 149.

With creative manipulation of perspective, an image can appear to be 3-dimensional.

STAR SEARCH

Of the shapes pictured below, which one does not belong?

Answer on page 150.

TWIRLING PINWHEELS

No, these pinwheels aren't actually moving—though they sure seem like they are!

AUTHOR! AUTHOR!

This illusion is another example of the subtleties that can be achieved with simple lifework, specifically how ours mind fills in gaps to create a consistent image. Hidden below is the writer of this evening's production, somewhere very unexpected. You won't see him at first, because he doesn't naturally appear. But when you do spot him, he'll become the focus of the illustration.

Answer on page 150.

TUBES WITHOUT END

Focus on the tubes below as they turn and turn and turn...

How many things can you find that start with the letter N? Finding 9 would be NICE. Finding 19 would be NOTHING short of stupendous!

Answer on page 150.

Stare at these spirals—do they appear to move?

It looks like these colors are bursting off the page!

OPTICAL PUZZLES

Complete the optical illusion and make it pop by coloring the areas that correspond to the numbers in the color key. Use our color suggestions, a light-medium-dark combination of your own, or any other three colors you like.

Answer on page 150.

Oops! Four mugshots accidentally got sent through the shredder, and Officer Burns is trying to straighten them out. Currently, only one facial feature in each row is in its correct place. Officer Burns knows that:

      1. C's nose is one place to the left of D's mouth.

      2. C's eyes are one place to the right of C's hair.

      3. B's nose is not next to C's nose.

      4. A's eyes are 2 places to the left of A's mouth.

      5. C's eyes are not next to A's eyes.

      6. D's hair is one place to the right of B's nose.

Can you find the correct hair, eyes, nose, and mouth for each person?

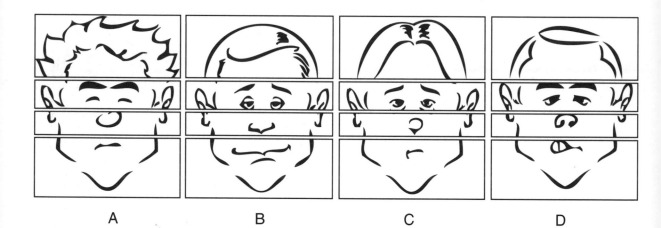

A   B   C   D

Answer on page 150.

SPINNING ZIG, TURNING ZAG

Sure, these shapes are locked into their positions on the page, but that doesn't stop them from at least appearing to move!

MONKEY BUSINESS

This is clearly a picture of a monkey, wouldn't you agree? But maybe there's something more going on here. Maybe if you turn the page upside down, you'll be facing something unexpected…

If the area of the big square is 1, what is the area of the small square in the middle?

A. $\frac{1}{4}$

B. $\frac{1}{5}$

C. $\frac{1}{6}$

D. $\frac{1}{7}$

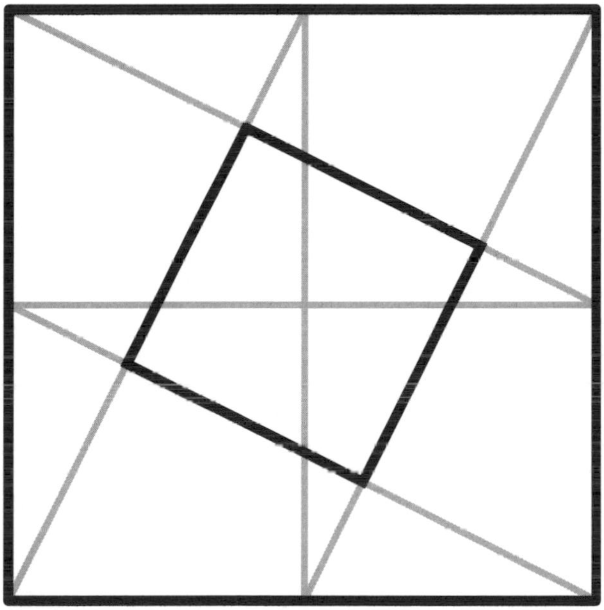

Answer on page 151.

If this triangle is cut along the dotted lines, can the four sections be arranged to form a perfect square? No need to use a protractor to solve this puzzle. We think you can do it with just your eyes.

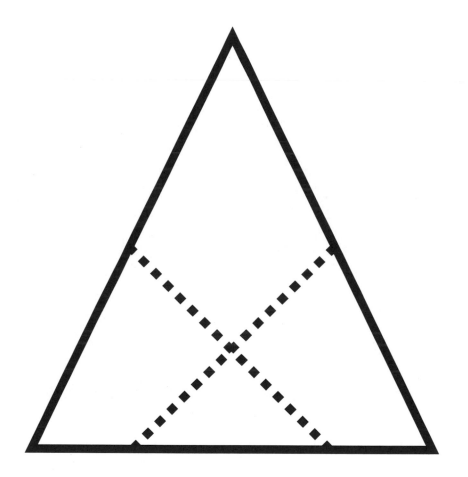

Answer on page 151.

Nope, this shape isn't coming off the page, it just appears to be. Thanks to perspective and space manipulation, these circles appear to be on the rise.

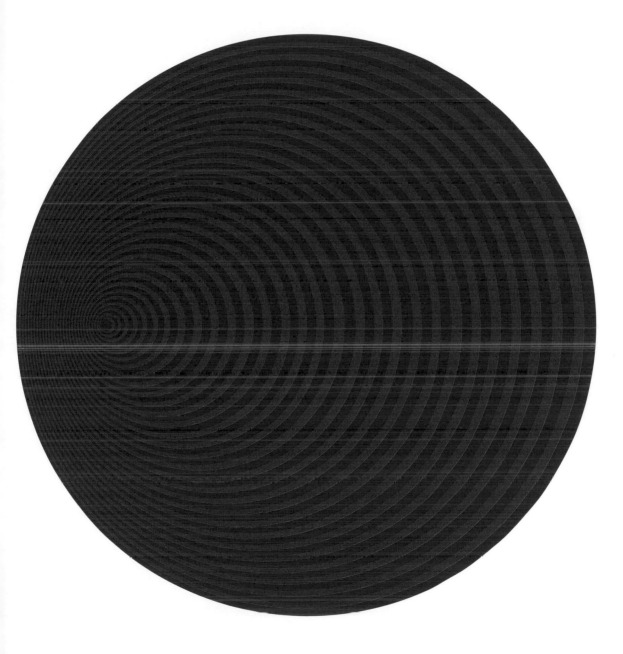

Take a look at this image. What happens to the white circles? They should turn to gray.

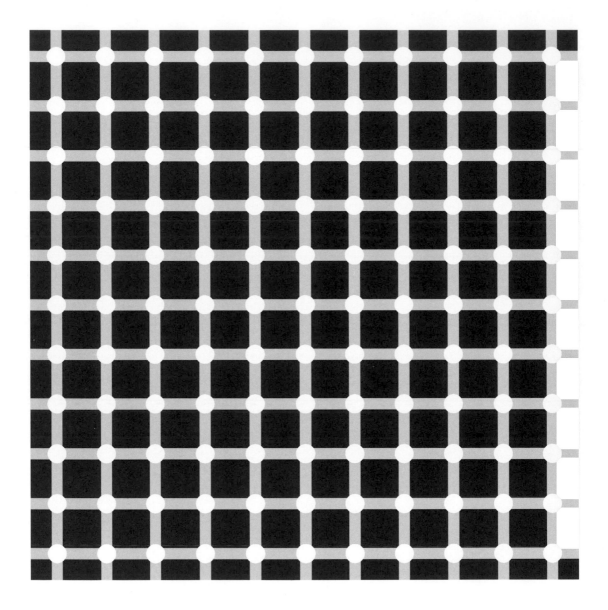

Making cuts along the grid's lines only, is it possible to divide a 5 x 5 checkerboard into 2 parts so that each part contains an equal number of light and dark boxes?

Answer on page 151.

OPTICAL PUZZLES

Complete the optical illusion and make it pop by coloring the areas that correspond to the numbers in the color key. Use our color suggestions, a light-dark combination of your own, or any other two colors you like.

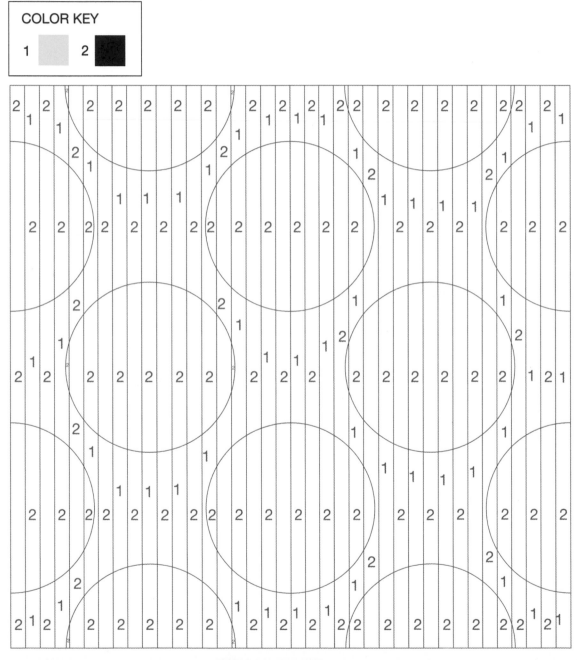

Answer on page 151.

When joined together without overlapping, will these 2 pieces form a perfect circle?

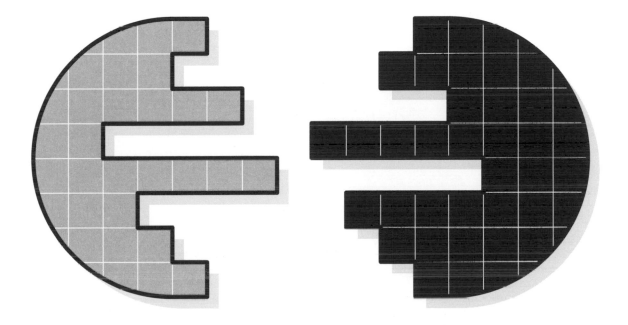

Answer on page 151.

This image, no matter how you look at it, cannot exist in the real world.

DRAWING THE LINE

Believe it or not, but hidden in this line illustration is a cat. Can you pinpoint Kitty's secret location?

Answer on page 152.

Try to keep your perspective while gazing at these twirling circles.

Which of these flowers has the longest stem?

Answer on page 152.

Which interior circle is larger?

Answer on page 152.

Get your bearings as you take a spin through these seemingly moving circles!

LINGERING IMAGE

We have a task for you: Stare at this skull for 30 seconds. Then, look at a white sheet of paper. What do you see?

Answer on page 152.

Don't be fooled here—those spinning discs only give the illusion of movement.

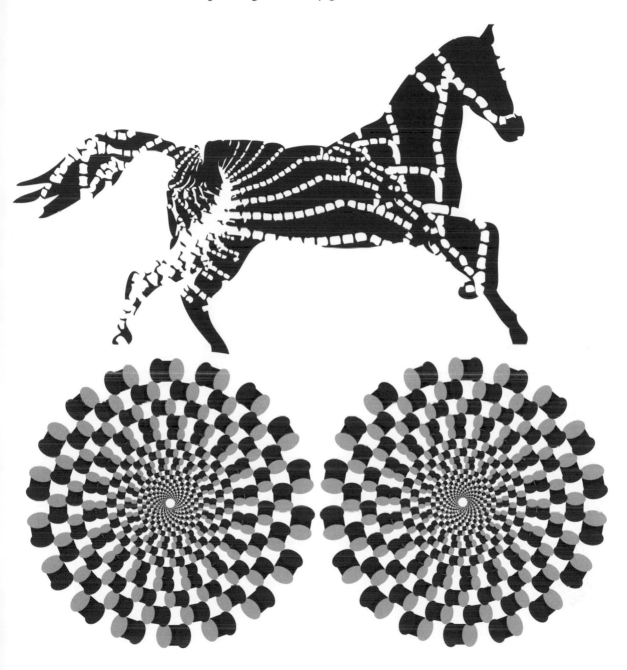

IDENTITY PARADE

Mrs. Amnesia was asked to recollect the faces of the 4 suspects who robbed the local bank. Her memory is a bit shaky though. The photos accidentally got put through a shredder, and, currently, only one facial feature in each row is in its correct place. Mrs. Amnesia does know that:

1. B's nose is not next to C's nose.
2. B's hair is one place to the right of B's nose.
3. B's eyes are one place to the right of B's mouth.
4. A's hair is one place to the left of D's mouth.
5. B's eyes are not on the same face as C's nose.
6. C's eyes are one place to the left of C's nose.

Can you find the correct hair, eyes, nose, and mouth for each suspect?

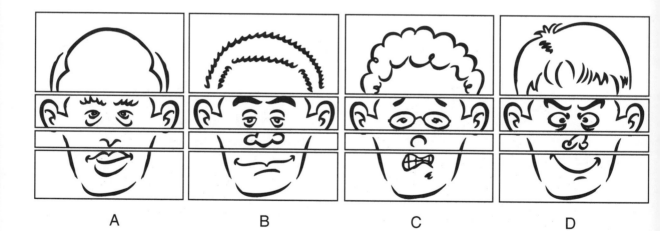

A   B   C   D

Answer on page 152.

Which line is longer, A or B?

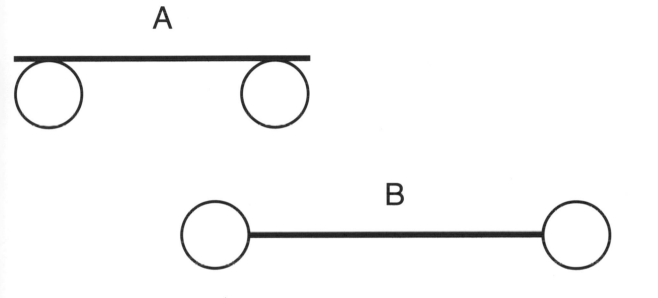

Answer on page 152.

If you let your eyes roam this image, you're likely to experience a warping affect. This is known as "anomalous motion," a term used to define the appearance of motion in a static image. Color contrasts and eye movement contribute to relative motion effects.

Complete the optical illusion and make it pop by coloring the areas that correspond to the numbers in the color key. Use our color suggestions, a light-medium-dark combination of your own, or any other three colors you like.

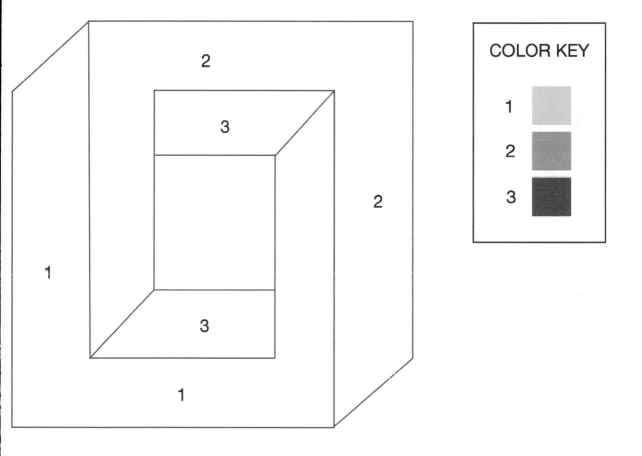

COLOR KEY

1

2

3

Answer on page 153.

MONDRIANIZE IT!

Inspired by the artwork of Belgian artist Piet Mondrian, these puzzles consist of stars and circles. Using the checkered pattern as a guide, draw in lines so that each star is in its own square, and each circle in its own rectangle.

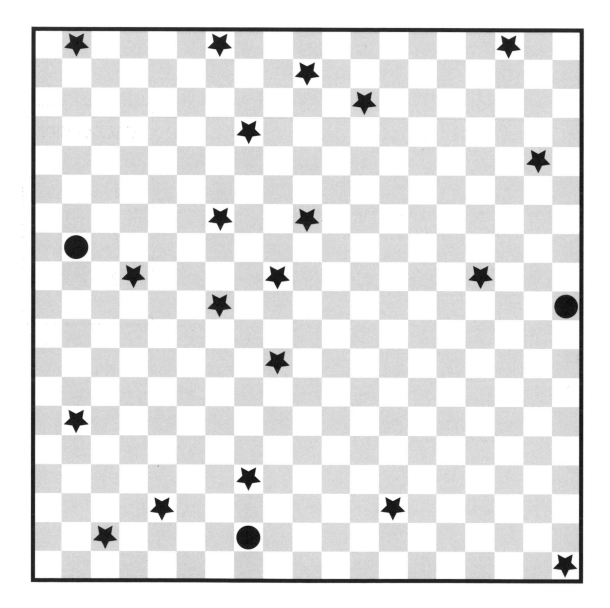

Answer on page 153.

How many 90-degree angles are hidden in this image?

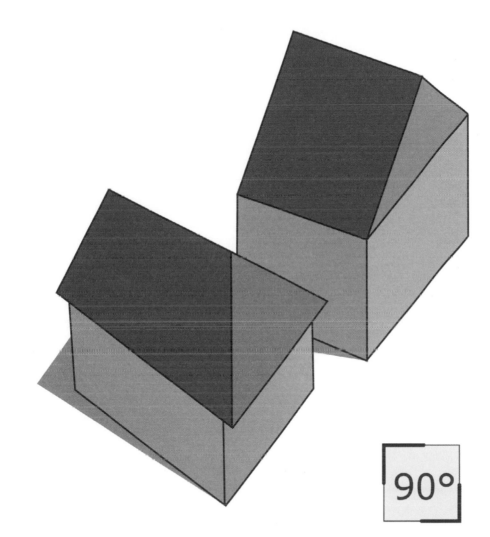

90°

Answer on page 153.

Something's wrong with the math here. There are 3 bunnies, but only 3 ears. Yet this image seems on the up-and-up. At closer study, the trick becomes evident - these bunnies are sharing ears.

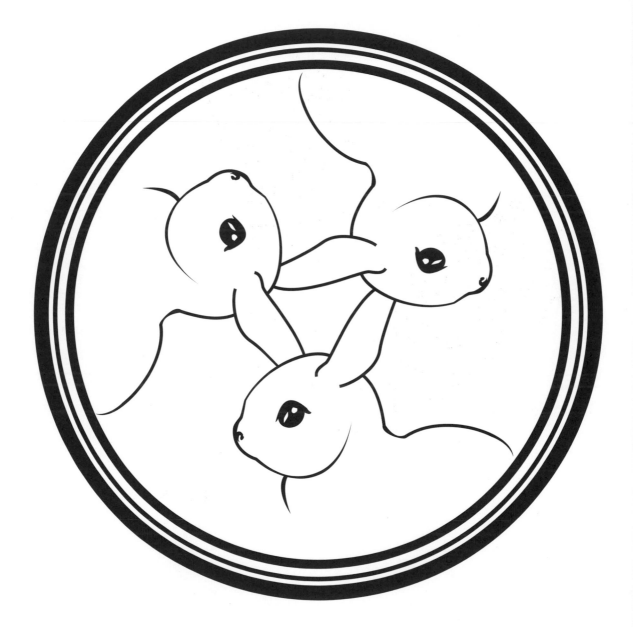

PARADE'S ROUTE

The parade starts at the top left corner, visits each street corner exactly once, and ends back at the same corner it started on. Can you draw in the parade's route?

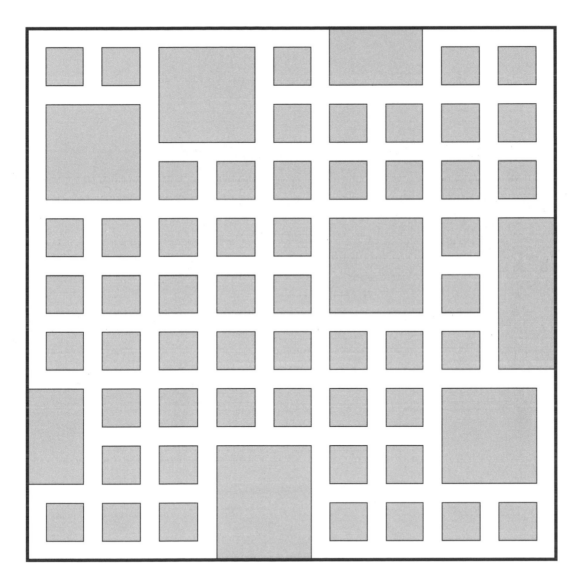

Answer on page 153.

PYRAMID LINES

Are lines A and B the same length?

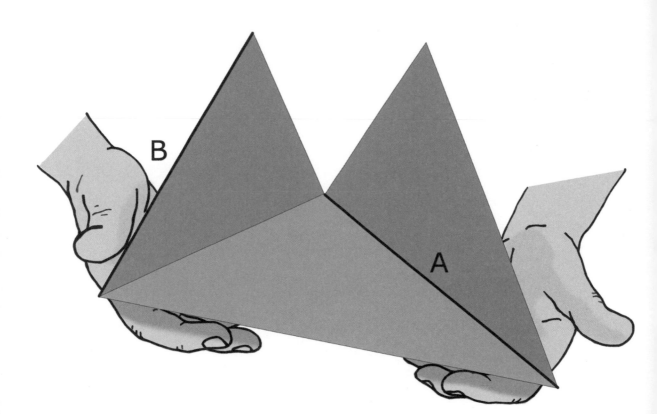

Answer on page 154.

SHADES OF GRAY

Take a look at this image—seems like there are multiple shades of gray, right? Actually, there are only 2 shades used. Colors seem darker or lighter depending on the colors they are surrounded by.

Complete the optical illusion and make it pop by coloring the areas that correspond to the numbers in the color key. Use our color suggestions, a light-medium-dark combination of your own, or any other three colors you like.

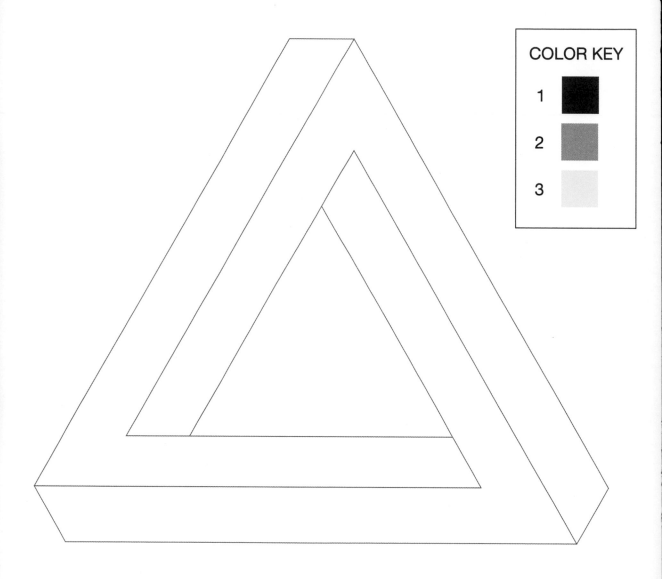

COLOR KEY

1

2

3

Answer on page 154.

JAGGED LINES

Try to follow the black and white lines in this image. Having trouble? The lines aren't continuous—they only appear to be due to a trick of the shapes and colors.

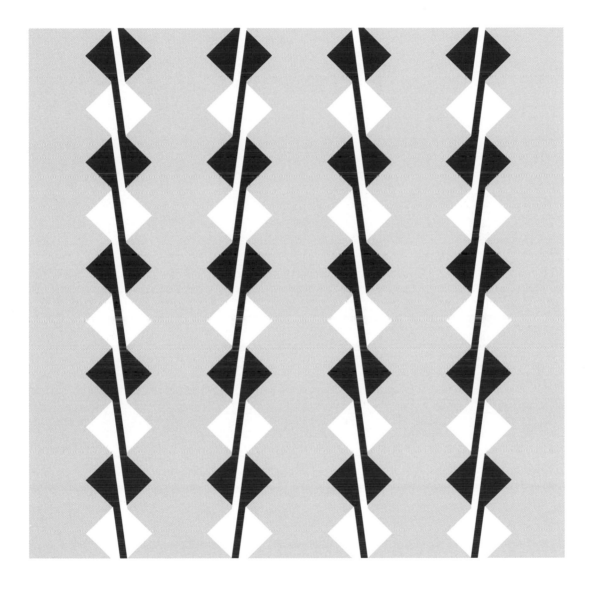

Begin by looking at this puzzle at a normal reading distance. Slowly, move the page closer to your face. As you do, you'll see the bird find his way home.

Which choice belongs in the last circle?

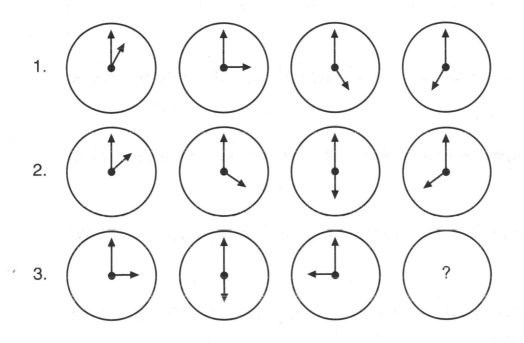

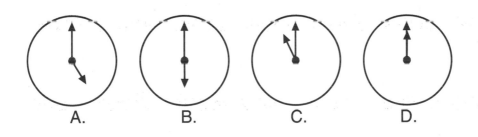

A.   B.   C.   D.

Answer on page 154.

BAMBOO EFFECT

Notice the shades of gray running within the yellow bamboos? They actually don't exist! The color within the bamboos is perfectly even; the illusion of the gray is induced by the surrounding gray tones. This is an effect of lateral inhibition.

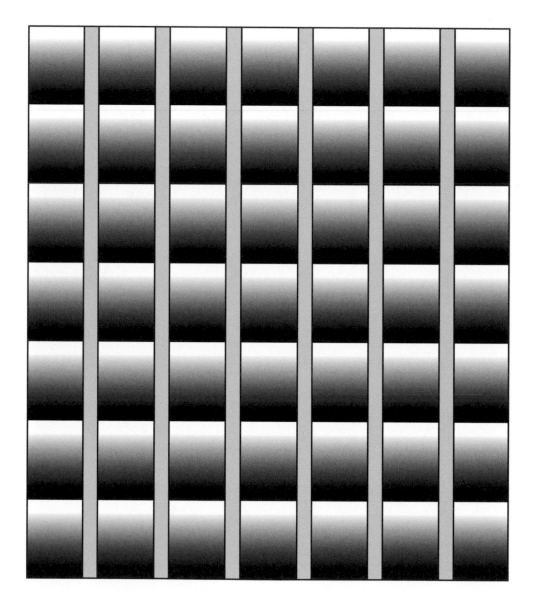

IMPOSSIBLE CUBE

These cubes stacked on cubes (or within cubes) is an impossible shape. It may look right at a glance, but this design couldn't be created, other than on paper.

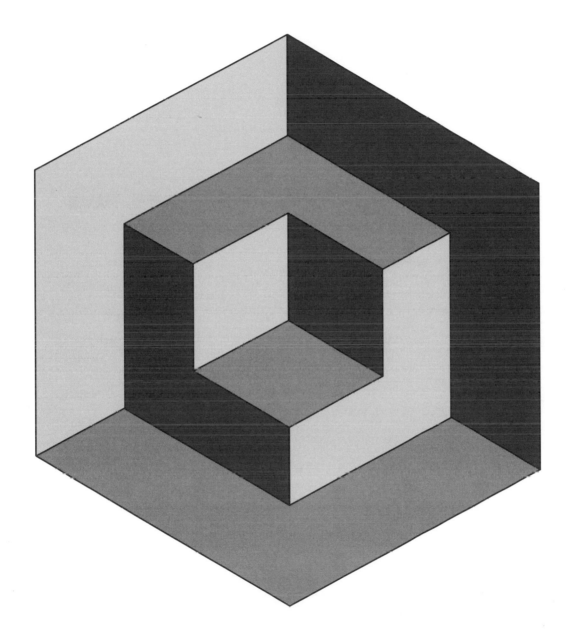

Only one of the cubes has the swimmers following the pattern of the flattened cube in the center. Which is it?

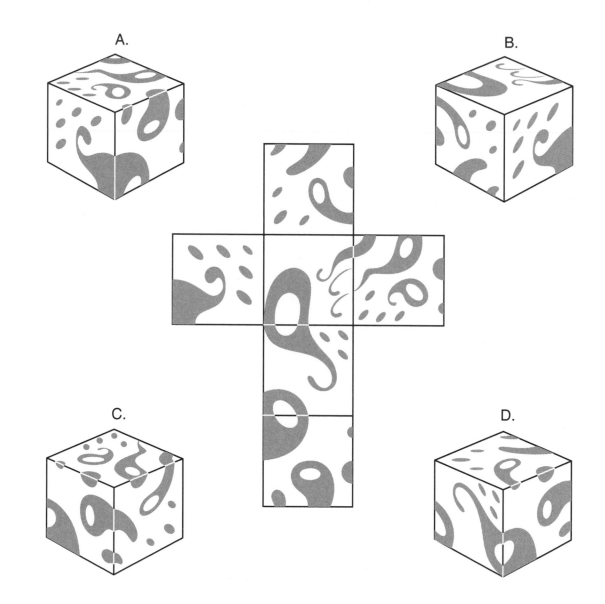

A.

B.

C.

D.

Answer on page 154.

Which piece of cheese (A, B, or C) is cut from the semicircle below?

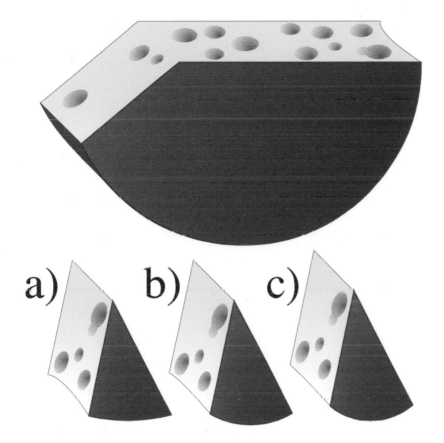

a) b) c)

Answer on page 154.

OPTICAL PUZZLES

Complete the optical illusion and make it pop by coloring the areas that correspond to the numbers in the color key. Use our color suggestions, a light-medium-dark combination of your own, or any other three colors you like.

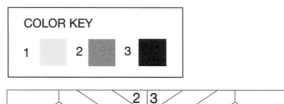

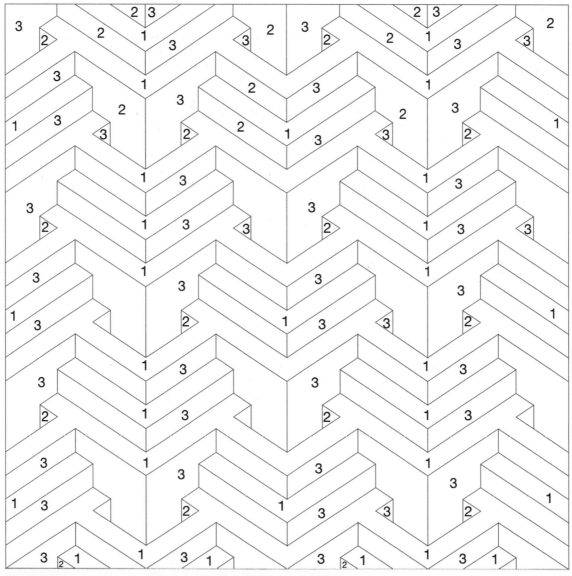

Answer on page 154.

WHICH WAY IS UP?

Are these tiles facing up or down? Also, study the top and bottom rows. The tiles aren't completely outlined; but, because the middles tiles are complete, your mind fills in the gaps.

HANDS HOLDING...?

The triangle below is not a triangle at all: The shape you see is an illusion created by the 3 hands and shaded points. The white is the exact same color as the background.

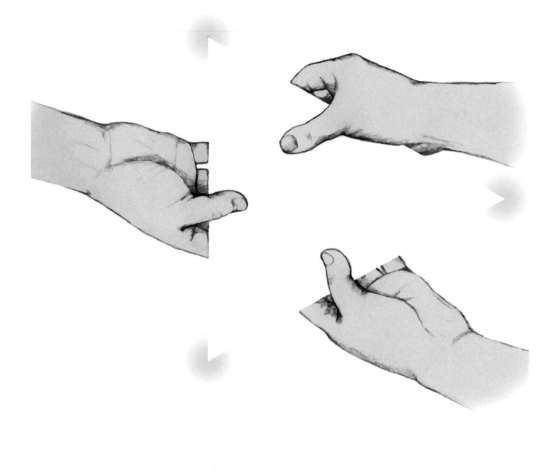

ARROW WEB

Shade in some of the arrows so that each arrow in the grid points to exactly one shaded arrow.

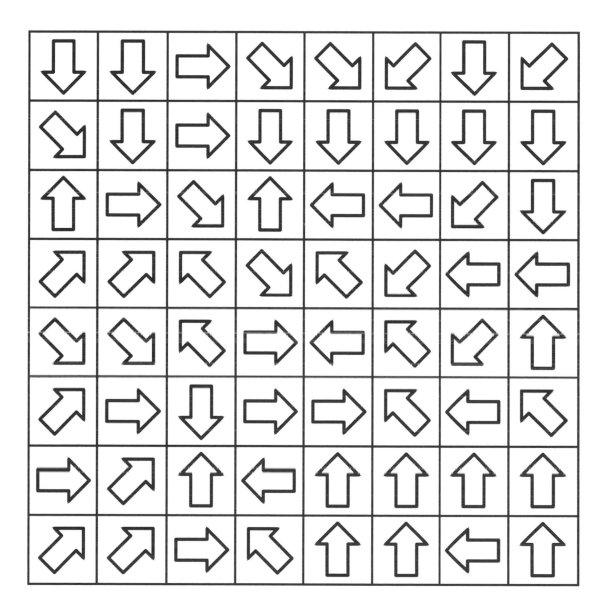

Answer on page 155.

Which color stripe, B or C, is an exact match for stripe A?

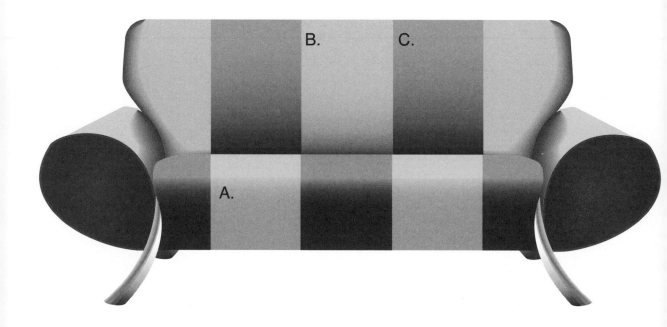

Answer on page 155.

Imagine you are driving and you see the reflection of this car in your rearview mirror. Can you read the message on the hood? What does it say?

Answer on page 155.

BROKEN HEART

Is it possible to divide the heart into 2 identical shapes by separating it only along the white grid lines?

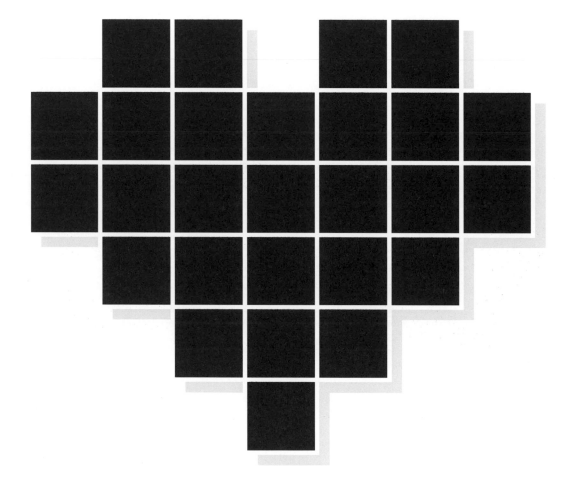

Answer on page 155.

OPTICAL PUZZLES

Complete the optical illusion and make it pop by coloring the areas that correspond to the numbers in the color key. Use our color suggestions or any other six colors you like.

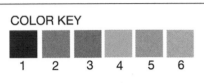

Answer on page 155.

MAX-DIE-SUM

What is the maximum sum of a common die's pips that can be seen simultaneously? No mirror or special tricks can be used.

Answer on page 155.

How many times does the letter F appear in this sentence?

Answer on page 156.

SWOLLEN ILLUSION

Take a good look at this image—not only does the center appear to extend outward, but something else is going on as well. After only a few seconds, white dots should form in the black lines. This is an afterimage effect.

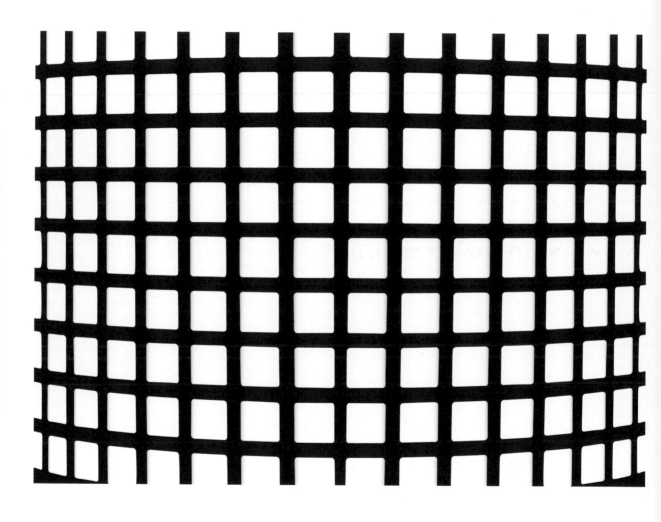

Oops! Four mug shots were accidentally sent through the shredder, and Officer Barry is trying to straighten them out. Currently, only one facial feature in each row is in its correct place. Officer Barry knows that:

1. C's eyes are one place to the left of his mouth.
2. B's mouth is not next to C's mouth.
3. A's nose is one place to the left of D's hair.
4. B's eyes are on the same face as A's mouth, and are one place to the right of B's hair.
5. B's nose is one place to the right of his mouth.

Can you find the correct hair, eyes, nose, and mouth for each suspect?

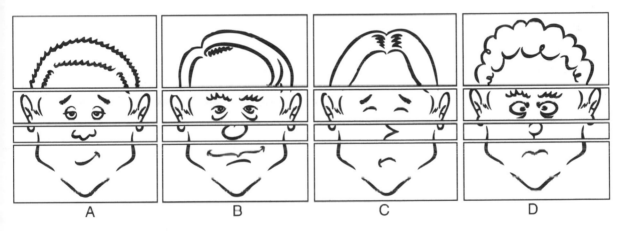

A   B   C   D

Answer on page 156.

RAINBOW BRIGHT

The colors in the top rainbow have completely faded. To brighen it back up, stare at the white dot in the bottom rainbow for 20 seconds, then shift your gaze back to the top rainbow. This illusion is based on color adaptation and afterimage effect.

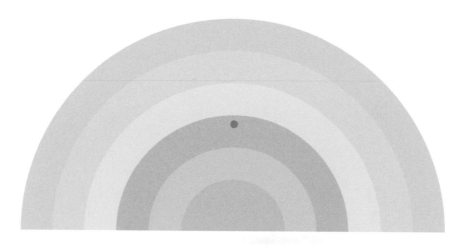

Concentrate on the black circle in the center. Hold your focus and watch the surrounding gray disappear.

Complete the optical illusion and make it pop by coloring the areas that correspond to the numbers in the color key. Use our color suggestion or any other color you like.

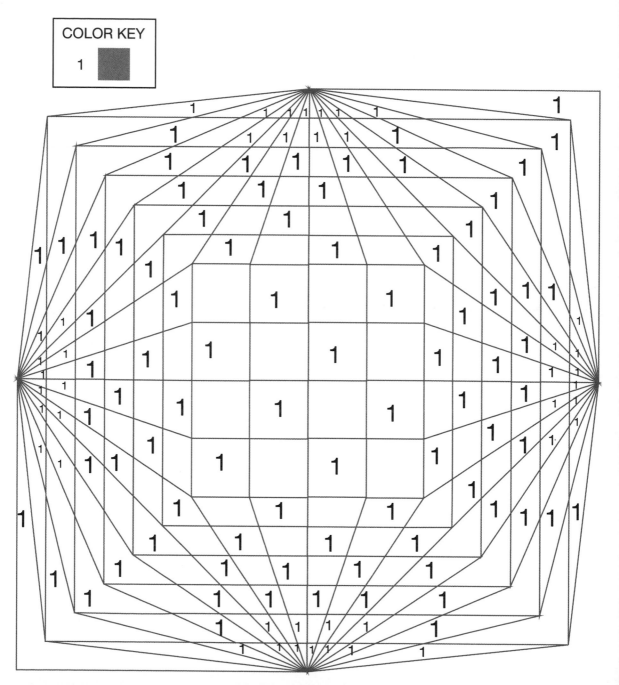

Answer on page 156.

ARROW WEB

Shade in some of the arrows so that each arrow in the grid points to exactly one shaded arrow.

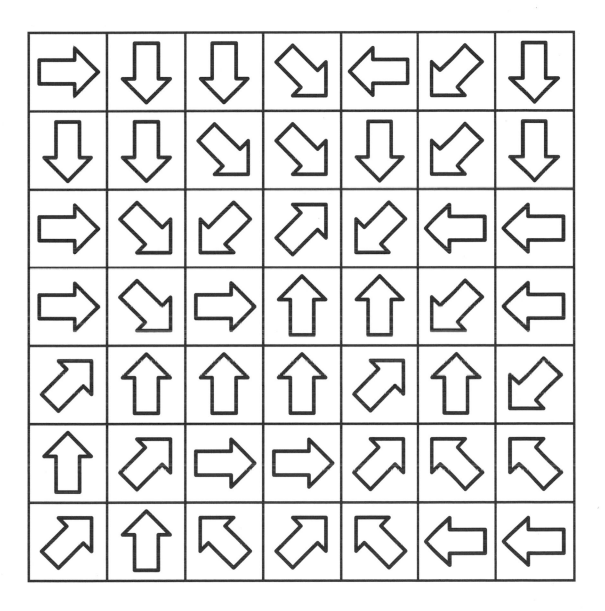

Answer on page 156.

THE PULSE

All is takes is a quick glance to see something unusual with this picture—namely that the lines appear to be pulsing. This is an illusion of design, created by how the lines are laid out.

Not so much. The lines only seem to be crooked, due to the opposing directions of the shapes they intersect.

DUCK COLOR

Recover the white color of this duck's plumage! To restore the color balance, stare at the X in the left diagram for 20 seconds, then shift your gaze over to the duck, specifically to the O in the right diagram.

How many things can you find that start with the letter P? Finding 40 would be Pretty darn good. Finding 45 or more would be almost Perfect!

Answer on page 156.

Look into the center circle and you'll see the sides of the square buckle inward.

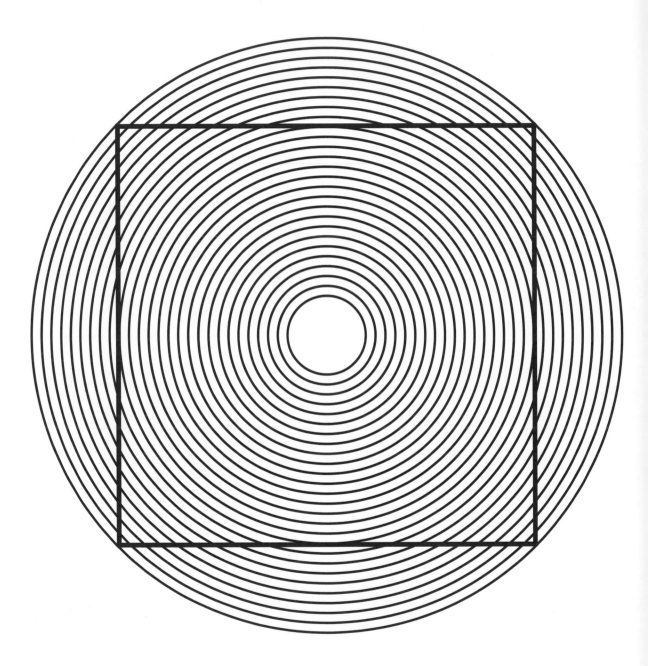

OPTICAL PUZZLES

Complete the optical illusion and make it pop by coloring the areas that correspond to the numbers in the color key. Use our color suggestions, a light-medium-dark combination of your own, or any other three colors you like.

Answer on page 157.

DOUBLE FACE

Do you see 2 faces, or 3? This kind of illusion, known as an "undecidable image," has been around since ancient times!

Answer on page 157.

RECORD PLAYER

Check out the circle below; if you stare at it long enough, it will appear to spin, like a record.

Which line is longer, red or blue?

Answer on page 157.

Which is the odd one out?

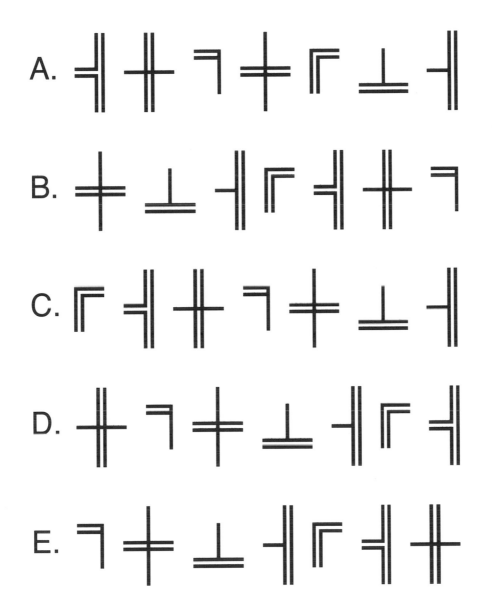

Answer on page 157.

Which interior square is darker, the one on the left or the one on the right?

Answer on page 157.

Which direction is this man facing?

Answer on page 157.

Which one of the cubes can be made from the unfolded sample?

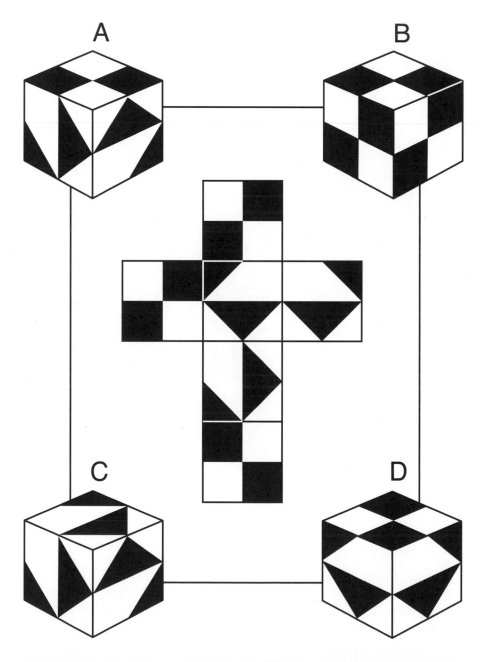

Answer on page 158.

Which of the 3 men depicted in this illustration is the tallest?

On which wall does the roaming dot appear? Inner? Outer? Depending on your perspective, it could be either!

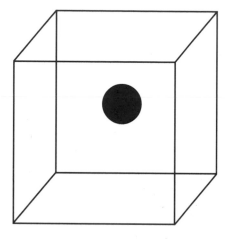

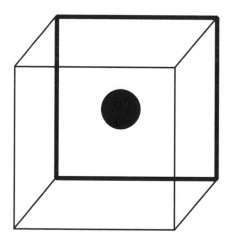

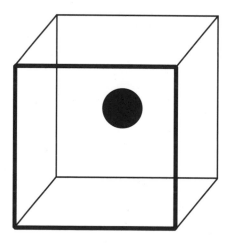

The parade visits each street corner exactly once and forms a complete circuit. Find the parade's route.

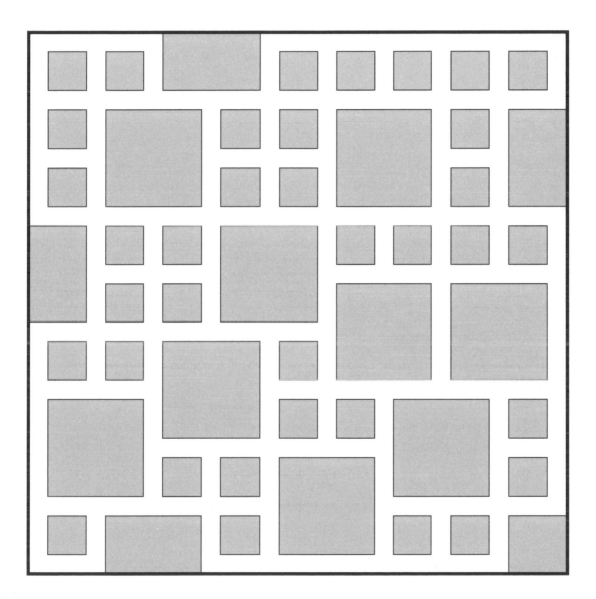

Answer on page 158.

Complete the optical illusion and make it pop by coloring the areas that correspond to the numbers in the color key. Use our color suggestions, a light-medium-dark combination of your own, or any other three colors you like.

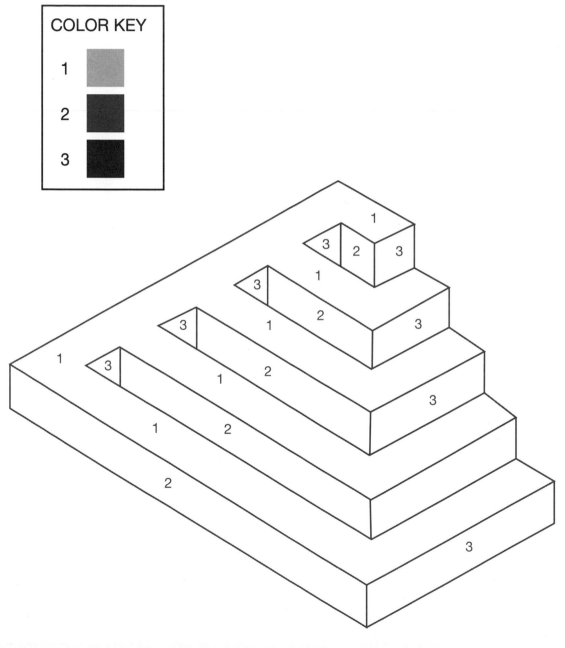

Answer on page 158.

Are each pair of letters in these typographical symbols the same size, or are they different?

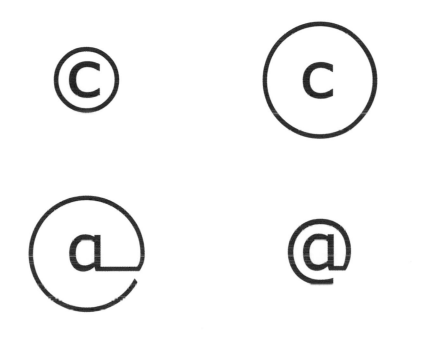

Answer on page 158.

What letter do you see here?

Answer on page 158.

Complete the optical illusion and make it pop by coloring the areas that correspond to the numbers in the color key. Use our color suggestions, a light-medium-dark combination of your own, or any other three colors you like.

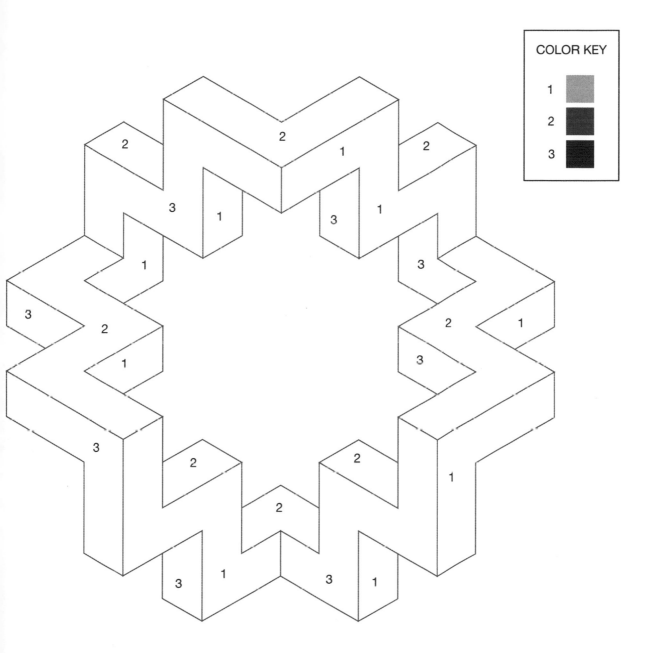

COLOR KEY

1

2

3

Answer on page 158.

Four folding patterns are scattered around the cube shown below. Determine the 2 patterns that form a cube when folded along the lines. No parts of each cube should overlap each other.

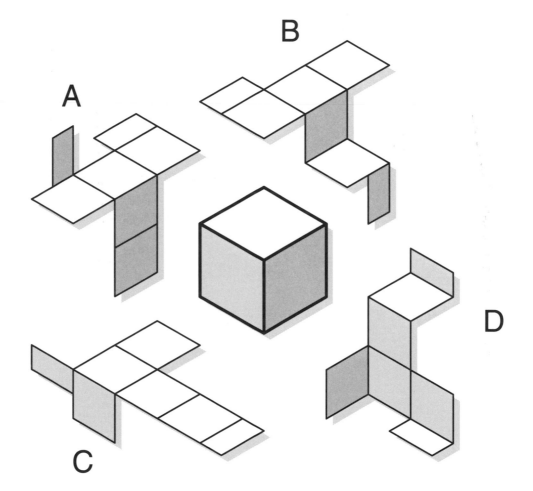

Answer on page 159.

Which line is longer, A or B?

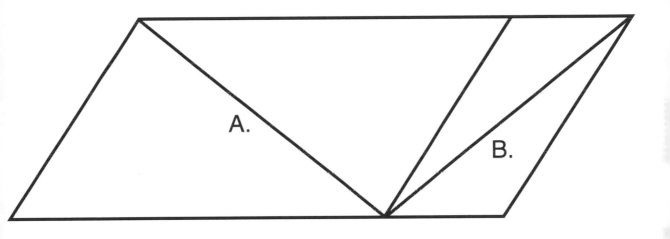

Answer on page 159.

MONDRIANIZE IT!

Inspired by the work of Dutch artist Piet Mondrian, this puzzle consists of stars and circles. Using the checkered pattern as a guide, draw in lines so that each star is in its own square, and each circle in its own rectangle.

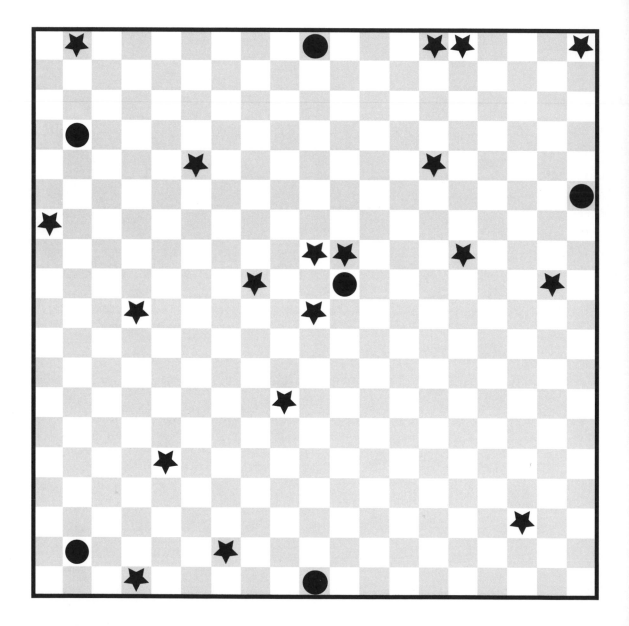

Answer on page 159.

DISTORTED SQUARES

Which of these squares is actually a proper, real square, A or B?

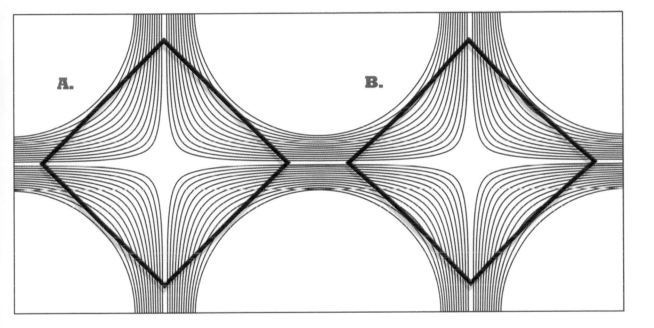

Answer on page 159.

Do you see a complete triangle or circles with triangles cut into them?

Shade in some of the arrows so that each arrow in the grid points to exactly one shaded arrow.

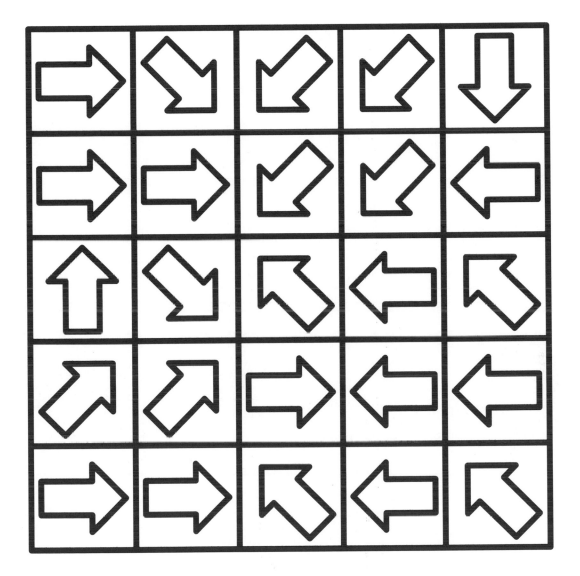

Answer on page 159.

At first sight, it seems that all the red lines on the left straw can be continued into the green and orange lines on the middle and right straws. Is that possible?

Answer on page 160.

Turn the page upside-down: What do you notice?

Sublime

Apache

Answer on page 160.

SPIRAL DESIGN

Both statues below (A and B) contain spiral designs. Statue B is a mirror image of A yet something is wrong. Can you spot the difference between the 2 statues?

Answer on page 160.

IDENTITY PARADE

Oops! Four mugshots accidentally got sent through the shredder, and Officer Wallers is trying to straighten them out. Currently, only one facial feature in each row is in its correct place. Officer Wallers knows that:

    1. C's nose is 1 place to the right of her mouth and 2 places to the right of D's hair.

    2. C's eyes are 2 places to the left of her hair.

    3. A's eyes are 1 place to the right of B's nose and 1 place to the right of D's mouth.

Can you find the correct hair, eyes, nose, and mouth for each person?

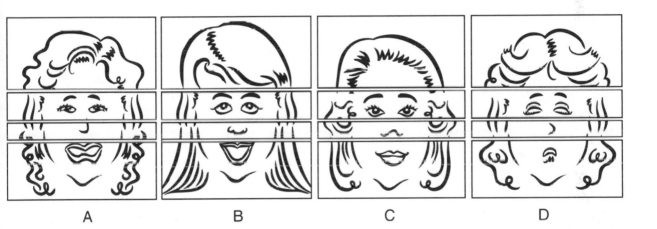

A   B   C   D

Answer on page 160.

Stare at this image long enough, and you'll see black dots appear in the white spaces.

SQUARE RINGS

Which ring has the bigger area, red or blue?

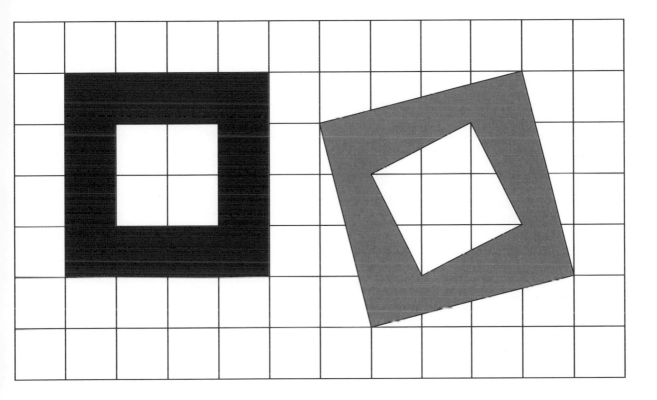

Answer on page 160.

Alternate Corners (page 5)

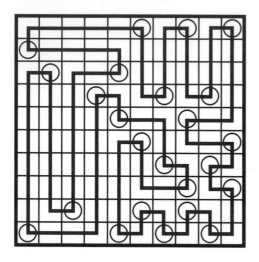

Square Holdings (page 7)

Aloha! (page 8)

1. She has 2 right feet; 2. she has 6 fingers on her left hand (counting the concealed thumb)

Optical Puzzles (page 6)

Mondrianize It! (page 9)

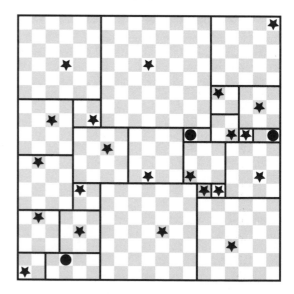

ANSWERS

Star Contrast (page 10)

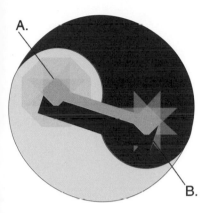

Catching Some Zs (page 11)

Roll the Dice (page 12)
Even though the red dot on the farther die seems much larger, it is the exact same size as the red dot on the closer die. The illusion is a trick of perception.

Curvaceous Cube Construction (page 13)
Answer is B.

Stepping Stones (page 15)

Arrow Web (page 17)

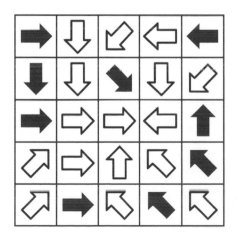

ANSWERS

Baaaffling Illusion (page 19)

Visual Sequence (page 20)
E. Each subsequent figure has one additional square.

Bookends (page 21)

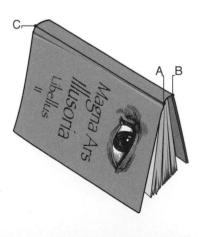

Optical Puzzles (page 23)

Identity Parade (page 24)

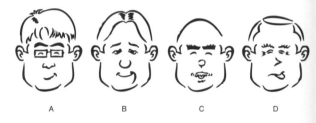

Find the Lovers (page 25)

ANSWERS

Parade's Route (page 26)

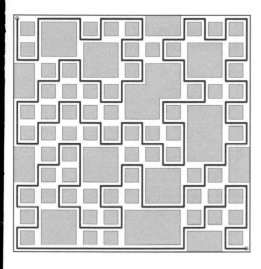

Line Difference (page 28)
They are the same size.

Divided Triangle (page 29)
B. 7

Triangles Galore! (page 30)
There are 14 triangles.

Optical Puzzles (page 32)

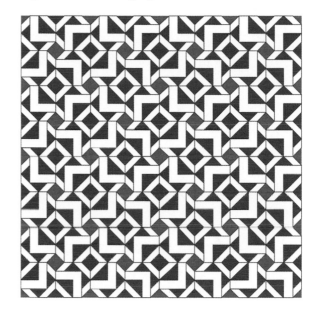

Flower Growth (page 35)

Height Times Width (page 36)
Though it appears the H is wider, they are the same width.

Square Donut (page 38)
There are 42 square outlines of 3 different sizes.

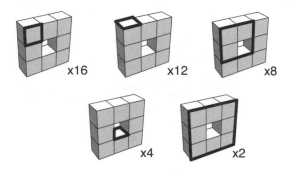

Optical Puzzles (page 39)

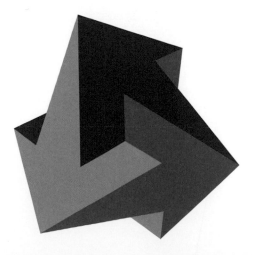

Up in Smoke (page 41)

Mondrianize It! (page 42)

ANSWERS

Optical Puzzles (page 46)

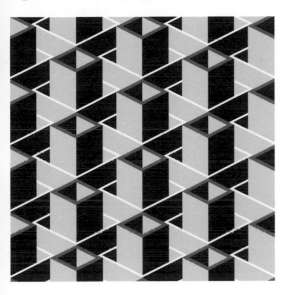

Don't Get Outfoxed (page 47)

It's a Wrap! (page 48)

The answer is B.

Optical Puzzles (page 50)

Star Search (page 52)

The other larger shapes all contain an amount of smaller shapes that are equal to their points.

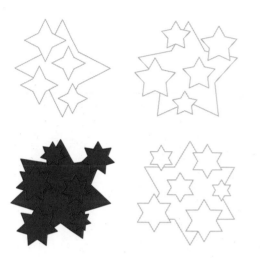

Author! Author! (page 54)

N Is for Nighttime (page 56)

Nail, neck (on boy), neck (on giraffe), nest, net, newspaper, Nick, nickel, nightstand, nighttime, nine, nine o'clock, nineteen, north (on compass), nose, notebook, notes, November, numbers, nutcracker

Optical Puzzles (page 59)

Identity Parade (page 60)

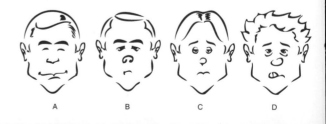

Square Area (page 63)

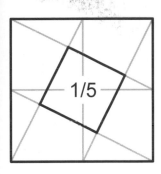

Triangle Cut (page 64)

5 x 5 Checkerboard (page 67)

No, it is not possible because each part must contain an even number of boxes, but this checkerboard has 12 light and 13 dark boxes.

Optical Puzzles (page 68)

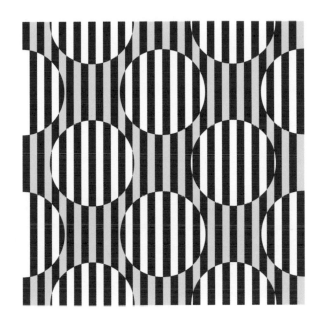

Perfect Circle (page 69)

No. These 2 pieces will form an oval, not a perfect circle.

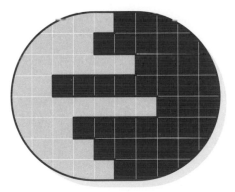

Drawing the Line (page 69)

Circular Studies (page 74)
They are the same size.

Lingering Image (page 76)
The skull appears on the sheet of paper, only the blacks and whites are reversed.

Identity Parade (page 78)

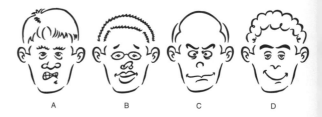

Connected Lines (page 79)
They are both the same size.

Flower Growth (page 73)

Optical Puzzles (page 81)

90 Degrees (page 83)

There are 8 angles. Most people locate 6, though there are 2 deceptive angles hidden between the houses. Some of the angles may not look like right angles, but this due to a trick of apparent perspective.

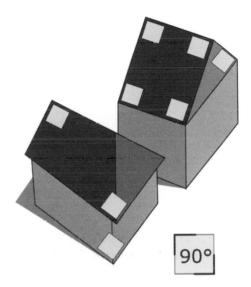

Mondrianize it! (page 82)

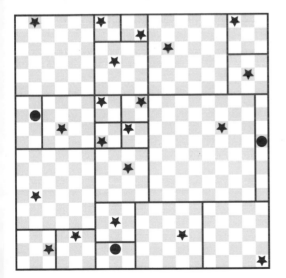

Parade's Route (page 85)

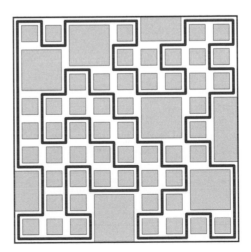

Pyramid Lines (page 86)
Yes.

Optical Puzzles (page 88)

Mind Stretcher (page 91)
D. In row 1, the times read 1, 3, 5, and 7. In row 2, the times read 2, 4, 6, and 8. In row 3, the times should read 3, 6, 9, and 12.

Swimming with the Cubes (page 94)
The answer is C.

Cheese Vision (page 95)

It would seem that B is that best fit, but the answer, when considering the exact angle and shape, is A.

Optical Puzzles (page 96)

Arrow Web (page 99)

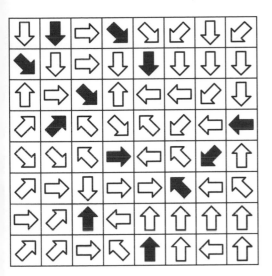

Comforting Illusion (page 100)

Though it seems incredible, A and C are exactly alike. A color always seems brighter when surrounded by dark colors, and vice-versa.

Front/Back (page 101)

This is an ambigram. Read one way, the letters read "front"; read another, they read "back."

Broken Heart (page 102)

No. There are an odd number of boxes (27), making an even split impossible.

Optical Puzzles (page 103)

Max-Die-Sum (page 104)

The maximum possible sum is 15 (4+5+6).

ANSWERS

Missing Fs (page 105)

Most people count 6 Fs, but there are actually 8! It's easy to glaze over the Fs in the preposition of—words such as "and," "from," and "of" are processed unconsciously by our mind.

Identity Parade (page 107)

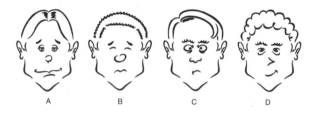

Optical Puzzles (page 110)

Arrow Web (page 111)

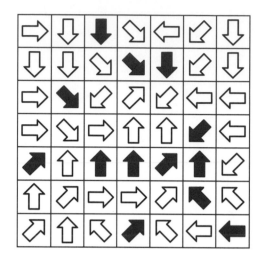

P Is for Preboarding (page 115)

Other answers are possible.

1. packages; 2. pad (of paper); 3. paddle; 4. pages; 5. pail; 6. palm (plant); 7. panda; 8. pants; 9. parachute; 10. parachutist; 11. Paris; 12. parka; 13. passenger; 14. passport; 15. pasta; 16. paws; 17. pear; 18. Pegasus; 19. pelican; 20. pen; 21. pencil; 22. people; 23. Peru; 24. Phoenix; 25. photos; 26. pickle; 27. pictures; 28. pie; 29. pig; 30. pigtails; 31. pile; 32. pilot; 33. pineapple; 34. pizza; 35. plaid; 36. plane; 37. planet; 38. plant; 39. plaque; 40. plate; 41. "Please Ship" sticker; 42. plow; 43. pocketbook; 44. polka dots; 45. pony; 46. ponytail; 47. popcorn; 48. postal worker; 49. poster; 50. pot; 51. president; 52. propellers; 53. pull-toy; 54. pump; 55. purse

ANSWERS

Optical Puzzle (page 117)

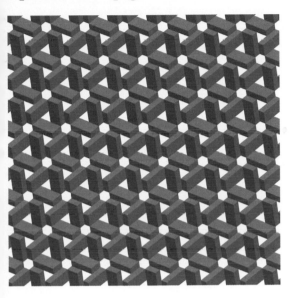

Double Face (page 118)
There are 3 faces—2 looking directly at each other, and a third created by combining the 2 sides.

Chopper Lines (page 120)
If you concentrate on the circle that surrounds the lines, the red one appears longer. But, if you concentrate on the helicopters instead, the blue one appears longer. The fact is that the blue is the longest of the pair.

Odd One Out (page 121)
A. The other symbols appear in the same order; they just start with a different symbol.

Center Squares (page 122)

Tricky Terrace (page 123)
There are 2 ways to perceive this image: from above (figure a.) or below (figure b.). These kinds of illusions are known as bistable figures.

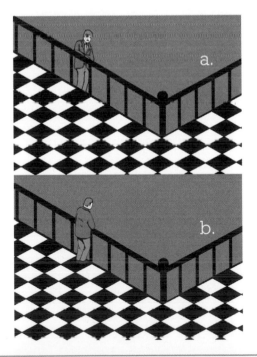

Geometric Cube Construction (page 124)
Answer is C.

Scholars (page 125)
The man in the foreground is actually 15 percent taller than the man in the background. .

Parade's Route (page 127)

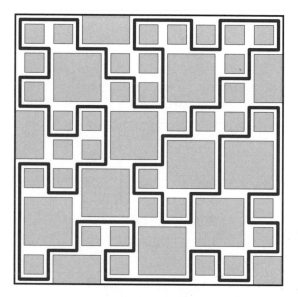

Optical Puzzles (page 129)

Copyrights (page 129)
They are all the same size. This illusion is known as an Ebbinghaus illusion.

Fractured Letters (page 130)

Optical Puzzles (page 131)

T-Cubed Rectangles (page 132)
Images B and C.

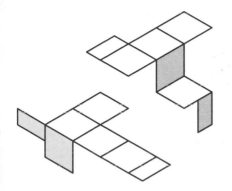

Parallelogram (page 133)
They are both the same size.

Mondrianize It! (page 134)

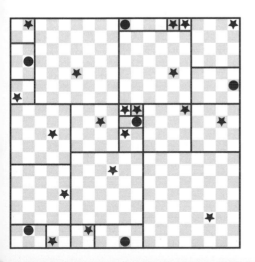

Distorted Squares (page 135)
Though most people say B, the answer is A! In cases of perception distortion, the brain interprets regular lines or shapes in the foreground incorrectly; those lines and shapes get contrasted to other lines and shapes in the background, making them appear distorted.

Arrow Web (page 137)

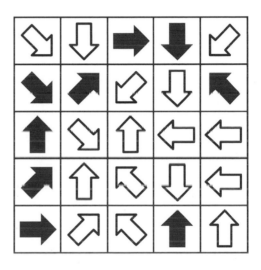

ANSWERS

Straw Alignment (page 138)
It is not possible. Only diagonal lines of the same color can be continuously linked together.

Ambigrams (page 139)
The words sublime and apache read exactly the same.

Spiral Design (page 140)
The spiral in statue A is actually 2 spirals, while the spiral in B is one spiral.

A. 2 spirals   B. 1 double spiral

Identity Parade (page 141)

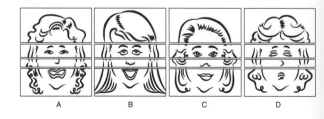

A   B   C   D

Square Rings (page 143)
Both have the identical area of 12 square units each.